I0098089

'Tis the Season

Experiencing the Comfort and Joy of *God with Us* when You're Single for the Holidays

Jessica Faith Hagen

Lilies & Sparrows
Publishing

Lilies & Sparrows
Publishing

Cover and Interior Design by Jessica Hagen / white paper background by Kiwihug via unsplash.com / octagon silhouette by Tree of Life App, used under creativecommons.org/licenses/by/4.0, changes made / purple paper photo by Heather Green via unsplash.com / orange material photo by Sincerely Media via unsplash.com / lights photo by Jack B via unsplash.com / snowflake graphic by Public domain vectors via unsplash.com / gift photo by Annie Spratt via unsplash.com / cookies photo by Prchi Palwe via unsplash.com / nativity photo by Ben White via unsplash.com

ISBN 978-0-9982353-7-0 (Paperback)
ISBN 978-0-9982353-8-7 (ebook)

Contents

Introduction

Ever since I first started writing about my journey of learning contentment in Christ in my singleness, I've wanted to write some sort of Christmas devotional/Bible study/book specifically for singles.

Because as a 34 year-old single woman, I've experienced many holiday seasons when my feelings about my singleness, and about being single during this season, were anything but merry and bright.

Rather, there have been many years when the holidays have brought with them an added weight to the heaviness of unfulfilled dreams; a stronger sense of loneliness; a more intense longing for the covenant and intimacy of marriage; a greater discouragement in being single longer than I had hoped; a deeper doubt of God's goodness and plan for me in the midst of unanswered prayers.

Friend, if you can relate to any of this, I'm glad you're here— and I'm not just saying that.

I'm glad you're here because I believe the discontentment, loneliness, disappointment, insecurities, and discouragement don't have to define our holiday season, or our singleness.

I believe our singleness can hold joy, hope, and so much goodness.

How?

In a word: *Jesus*.

After all, it is His birth that is the "reason for the season." And this reason doesn't hold any less joy, hope, and goodness for us in singleness than in romance and marriage. So this season doesn't have to hold any less joy, hope, and goodness for us when we're celebrating it as single people.

In these coming pages, I'll be sharing biblical truth, encouraging promises, practical advice, and some of my own story to help us embrace the joy, hope, and goodness of all we celebrate during this season, so that we can also embrace the joy, hope, and goodness God has for us in our singleness.

I've also included at the end of each chapter a Scripture reading, reflection questions, and a prayer.

I hope you read these words and are encouraged. I hope you read these words and feel seen. I hope you read these words and know you're not alone.

And mostly, I hope you read these words and remember God's heart for you: His heart that desires to comfort and care for you; to hold and uphold you; to fill you with joy and hope; to draw you closer to Himself—that you may see His glory, hear His voice, taste His goodness, sense His presence, and know His love.

Now before we begin, could I pray for you?

Dear Heavenly Father,

We come to You with expectant hearts. I ask that You meet the one reading this right where they are, in whatever heartache, loneliness, and discouragement they may be feeling in this season.

As they read these words and read Your Word, remind them of Your heart for them. Help them to know You see them, hear them, and are with them. Give them an assurance of Your love and care. Fill them with hope and joy. Show them Your glory and goodness.

We thank You for Your presence and Your promises. Draw near to us as we draw near to You.

Amen.

Praying for you + cheering you on,

Jessica Faith

Chapter 1
The Withness that Changes Singleness

It was Christmas time and I was at a family gathering, sitting with my chin in my hand and a smile on my face, taking in the conversation and laughter around me.

That's when they came up to me and made a show of examining my left-hand. Finding no ring, they theatrically made a face of shock, teasingly said something about me not having a boyfriend, then nudged my shoulder and asked with a chuckle, "What's wrong with you?"

As they turned away without even waiting for a response, my smile faded and I blinked rapidly to keep back the tears.

They may have been joking, but I was hurting.

And their insensitive teasing was like salt in a wound, because I already ached with the sorrow of still being single at the end of another year. I already throbbed with the loneliness of not having my person amidst all the people. I was already rubbed raw from the unmet longing to share my life, my heart, myself with someone who would call me theirs.

With all their wonder and magic, the holidays can have a way of magnifying the fact that we're *single*, as they bring closer proximity to the contrast of couples and families; a deluge of moments and memories we wish we were sharing with that person we could call "mine", and perhaps used to share with a spouse who is now gone; added to-dos we must handle solo; the gatherings and festivities we must navigate alone; and greater frequency of those questions and comments about our singleness that are at best annoying and at worst hurtful.

There's nothing wrong with being single. In fact, singleness abounds with beautiful and beneficial theological significance.[1]

I'll say it again: there's nothing wrong with being single. But there is stuff that's hard about being single. And our singleness can feel *not right* when we're longing for intimacy, support, and belonging, but instead feel lonely, left-out, and less-than.

How can we celebrate this season with joy and hope, when in this season being single feels hard and heavy, and maybe even hurts?

—

There's a name of God that has become more meaningful and encouraging to me the more I experience the holidays as a single woman.

That name is *Immanuel*, which means *God with us*.

We read this name and its definition in Matthew's telling of the Christmas story, where he quotes an Old Testament prophecy that was fulfilled in Jesus' birth:

"'The virgin will conceive and give birth to a son, and they will call him Immanuel' (which means 'God with us')." Matthew 1:23, quoting Isaiah 7:14

Throughout the Old Testament, we can read many promises from God to be with His people. Deuteronomy 31:8; Joshua 1:9; Isaiah 43:2; and Zephaniah 3:17 are just a few.

But the prophecy from Isaiah that Matthew quotes speaks of God becoming *incarnate*.

There are a few New Testament passages that speak of this *incarnation*, describing what it means and why it matters:

"Because God's children are human beings—made of flesh and blood—the Son also became flesh and blood... [I]t was necessary for him to be made in every respect like us, his brothers and sisters." Hebrews 2:14; 17, NLT

---

[1] One excellent book on the theological significance of singleness is *The Meaning of Singleness: Retrieving an Eschatological Vision for the Contemporary Church* by Danielle Treweek (InterVarsity Press, 2023)

"[Jesus], being in very nature God, did not consider equality with God something to be used to his own advantage; rather, he made himself nothing by taking the very nature of a servant, being made in human likeness." Philippians 2:6-7

In becoming incarnate, our God—the God of immeasurable glory, staggering grace, and perfect goodness—not only stepped into the messy brokenness of our world, but experienced it as a human, just as we do, Himself being broken and suffering for us:

"For only as a human being could [Jesus] die, and only by dying could he break the power of the devil, who had the power of death. Only in this way could he set free all who have lived their lives as slaves to the fear of dying... Since he himself has gone through suffering and testing, he is able to help us when we are being tested." Hebrews 2:14-15; 18, NLT

"And being found in appearance as a man, [Jesus] humbled himself by becoming obedient to death—even death on a cross!" Philippians 2:8

This is what Christmas celebrates: Jesus' brith; God incarnate; the Word become flesh (Jn. 1:14). God coming to us in our suffering, our brokenness, our sin, so that we could be saved, healed, and restored in relationship with Him.

In the incarnation, we see that the *withness* of *God with us* isn't just a coming alongside or being next to—it is a uniting of Himself to us, so we could be united with Him in a loving and holy relationship (Heb. 2:10-12).[2]

Immanuel, truly *God with us*.

—

There is Someone who calls us *His*:

- His child (1 Jn. 1:3)
- His treasure (1 Pet. 2:9)
- His temple (1 Cor. 3:16-17)
- His bride (Rev. 19:7-8)

---

[2] Samuel M. Powell, *The Trinity* (The Foundry Publishing, 2020), 59-60

- His witness (Acts 1:8)
- His beloved (Eph. 1:4)
- His workmanship (Eph. 2:10)
- His co-heir (Rom. 8:17)
- His body (Rom. 12:5)
- His friend (Jn. 15:15)

There is Someone we can call *mine*:

- my Savior (Tit. 3:4-5)
- my Lord (Eph. 4:5-6)
- my Rock (Ps. 18:2)
- my Hope (Rom. 5:13)
- my Light (Eph. 5:8)
- my Joy (1 Pet. 1:8)
- my Friend (Jn. 15:15)
- my Father (Rom. 8:15)
- my Creator (Eph. 2:10)
- my Provider (Phil. 4:19)
- my Refuge (Ps. 46:1)
- my Shepherd (Ps. 23:1)
- my Love (1 Jn. 4:16-17)

Our Triune God: who from the beginning has come to us, pursuing us in His love, drawing us in His kindness, calling us in His grace, so that we could come to Him in repentance, freedom, and worship, and have relationship *with Him*.

This *withness* changes singleness.

This truth of who God is, that He is *God with us*, that He desires to name us as "His" and for us to call Him "mine", that He actually made the way for us to have union and communion with Him, that He is an intimate, personal, relational God—this transforms singleness from less-than, lacking, and lonely, to abundant with goodness, blessing, and belonging, as we'll continue to explore in the coming chapters.

So while the holidays can have a way of magnifying the hard stuff of singleness, so too can the truth of *God with us* in the midst of what's hard and heavy be magnified, both in our singleness as an encouragement to our own hearts, and through our singleness as a testament to those around us.

For whatever our relationships status, in every season we can say and celebrate: *I am His, and He is mine.*

Read Matthew 1:18-25

What about being single is hard, heavy, or hurts in this season?

How does the truth of *God with us* encourage you in the hard and heavy things?

Do you believe God calls you His? On pages 8 and 9 are listed some of what God calls us as His. Can you think of anything else? Which one do you need to believe and rest in this season?

On page 9 are listed some descriptions of who God is for us. Can you think of any others? Who do you need to remember God is in this season?

Dear Immanuel, thank You for always being with me, and for making the way for me to be with You. Help me to look to, lean on, and rest in You as my _____ this holiday season and always. Help me to live as Your _____ this holiday season and always. I love You and praise You. Amen.

Chapter 2
It's Okay to Cry

Joy is found all throughout the Gospel tellings of Jesus' birth:

A baby leaps for joy in his mother's womb (Lk. 1:39-44).

A song of joy bursts from the lips of a young woman (Lk. 1:46-55).

Neighbors share in the joy of a woman who was said to be barren bearing a child (Lk. 1:57-58).

An angel announces good news of great joy to shepherds in a field (Lk. 2:8-14).

Those shepherds rejoice upon seeing a Newborn wrapped in cloths and lying in a manger, just as the angel had said (Lk. 8:15-20).

Magi are overjoyed when their journey following a star finally brings them to the Child born to be King (Matt. 2:1-12).

Simeon and Anna rejoice at seeing the Baby they know is the promised Messiah (Lk. 2:25-38).

Indeed, the Birth of Christ is a joyous event, and it is something for us to celebrate!

And yet, even as the lights twinkle and the songs are sung and the Christmas story is read, there's a lot of emotions we may be feeling in our singleness that aren't so holly-jolly: sadness about being single in a season we wish we were sharing with that person we could call "mine"; disappointment of another year going by without our dreams coming true; feeling left out and overlooked amidst the focus on couples and families with children; stress and weariness with handling added to-dos by ourselves; heartache that a relationship we were in didn't last as we had hoped; frustration and hurt as yet another relative comments about our singleness but doesn't bother to listen to our hearts… and I could go on.

Because these feelings are heavy and hard and not pleasant to experience, it's easy to believe we shouldn't be experiencing them at all.

After all, isn't this time supposed to be a time of celebration and joy, of gratitude and enjoying God's gifts, of peaceful moments and heartwarming traditions and fun festivities?

Is there space for sadness and disappointment and frustration and weariness and pain?

—

Joy is found all throughout the story of Jesus' birth. Yet even as a star twinkles and songs are sung and a promised Baby is born, I'm sure there were a lot of emotions being felt that weren't all "peace on earth."

Zachariah and Elizabeth had prayed for years for a child, until all hope seemed gone, and they probably experienced much sorrow as year after year went by without their prayers being answered (Lk. 1:5-25).

Joseph was confused and conflicted about what to do when he found out his virgin betrothed was with child, and he may have felt hurt and betrayed by this as well (Matt. 1:18-19).

The shepherds were terrified when the angel of the Lord first appeared to them (Lk. 2:8-9).

Mary was troubled at the angel Gabriel's words of greeting, and she likely felt scared even as she submitted to God's will. Then she immediately visited her cousin Elizabeth, perhaps needing comfort and support during a time that could have felt lonely and overwhelming (Lk. 1:26-40).

Simeon and Anna came closer to the end of their lives than the beginning as they waited for God's promises to them to be fulfilled. During that waiting, they probably felt discouraged and tempted to give up at times (Lk. 2:25-37).

Sadness, disappointment, frustration, weariness, pain… it's all there.

And it was in the midst of this sadness, disappointment, frustration, weariness, and pain that our Savior came.

Our God is a God of compassion (2 Cor. 1:3), and we see this no better than in the incarnation, when Jesus who "being in very nature God" was born as a human Baby—fully God and fully Man (Phil. 2:6-7).

As a man, Jesus experienced life as we do, yet never sinned (1 Pet. 2:22); He suffered loss and pain (Matt. 14:9-13, 27:27-31; Jn. 11:1-35); His body became hungry and tired (Lk. 4:2, 8:23); He was misunderstood and insulted (Lk. 11:14-16; Jn. 10:22-39; 1 Pet. 2:23); He at times needed some time away from people (Lk. 5:16); He was concerned for His family and friends (Lk. 22:31-32; Jn. 19:26-27; Lk. 11:20-33). And while He was never controlled by His emotions, He certainly felt them—many similar to those felt by others during the events leading up to and surrounding His birth.

This is why only Jesus was able to go to the cross to die in our place: because He is fully God, perfect in love, power, and goodness; and because He is fully Man, born into this fallen world and growing, living, suffering, feeling as a human *with us*.[1]

—

It's okay to feel all the feels that come with being single for the holidays: both happy in the celebrations, and sad over a dream that hasn't come true; both grateful for family and friends, and lonely; both excited for the festivities, and stressed over all you have to do; both delighting in your favorite traditions, and longing to make new traditions with a spouse and children.

It's okay to feel it all, and you can have joy in it all. Because Jesus is *with* you in it all.

He hasn't abandoned you because of what you're feeling. He isn't aloof to the emotions you're experiencing. He isn't unseeing of your tears or unhearing of your cries.

Rather, He desires to comfort and care for you. Not in a way that downplays how you're feeling, telling you to "just be grateful for what you have," but in a way that compassionately understands and graciously holds space and lovingly embraces, saying, "I *know* this is hard and heavy. I'm here for you, *with you*. And it's okay to cry."

—

[1] Samuel M. Powell, *The Trinity* (The Foundry Publishing, 2020), 45-46, 59

Here are some ways we can rest in God's compassion and be held and upheld by Him when we're experiencing the hard and heavy emotions that come with being single over the holidays:

Pray

In the midst of ministry and miracles and living life as a human, Jesus "often withdrew to lonely places and prayed" (Lk. 5:16). And on the night He would be betrayed and arrested, "in agony of spirit" He prayed, "Father, if you are willing, please take this cup of suffering away from me. Yet I want your will to be done, not mine" (Lk. 22:42, 44, NLT)

In the midst of our heartache, sorrow, frustration, and other emotions, we can spend time with our Father in prayer. We can pour out our hearts to Him, honestly telling Him how we're feeling and offering our emotions to Him.

And in this pouring out of our hearts, we experience God's heart for us, as He comforts us with His love, as He convicts us of His truth, and as He cultivates us in His way.

Remember Truth

At the beginning of His ministry, Jesus was "led by the Spirit into the wilderness, where for forty days he was tempted by the devil. He at nothing during those days, and at the end of them he was hungry" (Lk. 4:1-2).

To say Jesus was hungry at the end of these forty days seems an understatement. He would have been famished. His stomach past the point of growling for food, and now just hopelessly hollow. And this says nothing of His mental and emotional state, which had to have been affected by the lack of food and the time alone in the wilderness.

And this is when the devil came to tempt Him.

I don't know about you, but when I'm experiencing sadness, loneliness, disappointment, or other overwhelming emotions, I'm much more vulnerable to believing the lies of the enemy telling me I'm worthless, I don't belong, there's no hope for my future.

Jesus resisted the temptation by submitting to and standing on the truth of God's Word (Lk. 4:1-13).

In the midst of our emotions, we need to remember the truth of who God is, of who we are in Christ, and of the life He promises to us and instructs us in living.

Remembering the truth of God's Word gives us a foundation on which to stand as we navigate the hard and heavy feelings and emotions.

Talk with Someone

On the night Jesus knew He would be betrayed, arrested, and condemned to die, He said to three of His disciples, "My soul is overwhelmed with sorrow to the point of death" (Matt. 26:38).

Even though the disciples didn't do a great job of being there for Jesus in this time of emotional anguish, Jesus still shared with them how He was feeling and invited them to stay near and support Him as He prayed (Matt. 26:36-44).

Whether it's with a trusted friend, someone wise we look up to, or even a professional counselor, sharing our sadness and struggles can help us process them, ease the burden, and release any shame around the emotions we're experiencing.

Prepare

If you know you're more prone to experiencing sadness (or other hard emotions) in your singleness over the holidays, you're in a good place. Because this means you can prepare for these feelings and emotions, and perhaps they won't be so overwhelming.

What does your mind, heart, and body need for processing these feelings during this season? What are some things you could do before, during, and after the holidays to help you navigate these feelings? (Prayer, remembering truth, and talking with someone are all great places to start!)

Let it Be Both

Enjoying this season and celebrating the "good news of great joy" (Lk. 2:10, CSB) that Christmas is all about doesn't mean we must manufacture a facade of holly-jolly-ness. This doesn't mean we must stuff our sadness or frustration or disappointment for the sake of being thankful and choosing joy.

It was "for the joy set before him" that Jesus "endured the cross" (Heb. 12:2), yet even with this anticipated joy of resurrection and redemption, as He endured the cross He still suffered sorrow, grief, pain, betrayal, and loneliness (Matt. 26:36, 27:46; Mk. 14:50; Lk. 22:47-48, 54-62).

Our experience of Christmas (and singleness) doesn't have to be *either/or*—it can be a season that's *both* hard *and* still full of joy.

—

None of these ideas are meant to be a quick fix for the hard and heavy emotions you may be experiencing (and they probably won't be).

I think we often want to rush through our emotions and get to feeling better a lot sooner than God does. Not that He doesn't want us to feel better; but more so, He wants to grow us in intimacy with Himself, and He can do that even in our sadness and disappointment and frustration and weariness and pain. And it's this intimacy—this *withness*—that is our comfort and joy in the midst of the hard and heavy emotions we're experiencing.

While your emotions may feel too heavy and overwhelming for you, they are not for God.

So whatever you're feeling, you can bring it to Him with honesty and without shame, because He comforts those who are sad; He encourages those who are disappointed; He calms those who are frustrated; He gives rest to those who are weary; and He holds close those who are hurting.

Read Matthew 26:36-46

What feelings and emotions do we see Jesus experiencing in this passage? Are there any that aren't explicitly stated but that you imagine He would have felt?

How do we see Jesus navigating these emotions?

What emotions are you experiencing in your singleness this holiday season?

On pages 15-16 are some ideas of ways we can rest in God's compassion when experiencing hard and heavy emotions. Which one do you want to practice this holiday season?

Dear Father of compassion, thank You for Your presence with me, even when I don't feel it. Right now, I'm feeling _____.
I offer these emotions to You, and ask that You would calm and comfort me, remind me of Your truth, and help me navigate these emotions in ways that are in line with Your heart. I love You and praise You. Amen.

Chapter 3
A Place of Still-ness

It's so close: Christmas Day.

In a blink it will be past, and we'll be ringing in the New Year.

Like many of you reading this, I've dreamed for practically my whole life of getting married and having kids. Like many of you, I've prayed (sometimes calmly and sometimes desperately) that God would guide me into this dream. Like many of you, I've waited (sometimes patiently and sometimes frustratedly) on His timing. Like many of you, I've hoped (sometimes confidently and sometimes despairingly) that each new year would be *the year* for this dream to come true.

Yet here we are: counting down the days 'til Christmas, coming to the end of the year, and still single.

Still dreaming, still praying, still waiting, still hoping.

And it's not easy coming to the end of a year, of *another year*, finding ourselves in this place of *still-ness*.

Because *stillness* means no movement: seemingly not getting any closer to those long-held, heart-held dreams; feeling like we're "falling behind" in life while everyone else's lives are moving forward past milestone after milestone; wondering when it will be our turn or if somehow we made a wrong turn that there's no turning back from.

For my whole adult life, my life has looked largely the same: I've been at the same job for 13-plus years; I've attended the same church; I've been part of the same Bible study group for over 10 years; I've participated in the same family gatherings and traditions; I've watched the same Christmas story be enacted by children on stage year after year after year.

And when year after year after year, those same dreams go unfulfilled, those same hopes go unmet, those same prayers go unanswered (even if your life hasn't been quite the "same" as mine), *still* can start to feel a lot like *stuck*.

As we come to the end of another year, how do we navigate the disappointment of *still* being single when we'd hoped and dreamed this year would end differently?

———

The account of Jesus' birth that's most often recited in Christmas pageants is found in the book of Luke. But this Gospel doesn't begin with the story of Jesus' birth. Rather, the first story found in Luke is about a priest named Zechariah and his wife Elizabeth.

In chapter 1, we learn that Zechariah and Elizabeth are old, and despite fervent prayers for a child, they have remained childless (vv. 7, 13).

Then we get to the part of the story that makes it a story to be told and retold: the angel Gabriel visits Zechariah while he is serving in the temple and announces to him that Elizabeth will conceive and give birth to a son, who they are to name John. This son will be a forerunner to the Messiah, to awaken hope and make ready hearts for His coming (Lk. 1:8-17).

And there it is: the happily ever after every good story must have.

But we mustn't forget that this story is a true story, and that one of its characters is a real, flesh-and-blood woman who before her prayers were answered, before her dream was held in her arms, before this gift was given, like Sarah (Gen. 18:11) and Rachel (Gen. 30:1-2) and Hannah (1 Sam. 1:5) before her, like so many women throughout history, suffered years of infertility.

We don't know what Elizabeth's life was like before this angelic announcement, but I imagine there were many years of *still-ness* for her... still dreaming, still waiting, still praying, still hoping.

And maybe she even came to place where her dreams held more grief than expectancy, where her prayers were made more of tears than of hope, where her waiting became resigned to the impossibility of it all.

Zechariah and Elizabeth did eventually get their dream. But even then, it was probably different than they had expected and desired. To chase a toddler as their joints stiffened? To guide a teenager as their eyesight failed? Did they even live long enough to see their boy become a man, to witness with joy and wonder all the angel spoke about their son coming to pass? And if they did, wouldn't they have also experienced the heart-rending grief of him being imprisoned and executed for boldly confronting the sin of the land's rulers (Mk. 6:17-20)?

Yes, I believe Zechariah and Elizabeth were well-acquainted with the disappointment of dreams not coming true and life not turning out how you'd hoped and finding yourself in a place of *still-ness*.

Yet the defining narrative of their story isn't disappointment.

Elizabeth's name means *God is my oath*,[1] and the name Zechariah means *God remembers*.[2] Both names speak of the faithfulness of God to His covenant. And it's this faithfulness that's the defining narrative of Zechariah and Elizabeth's story.

From the beginning, God has covenanted Himself to the people He created, committing Himself to a relationship with them in which He promises their well-being and flourishing, in which He promises the well-being and flourishing of all creation.

When people sinned—the first time and then time and time again—rather than forsaking the relationship, God throughout the Old Testament renews His covenant with His people and promises to send the Messiah to deliver them from the bondage of sin and bring them to a home of rest and abundance in Him.[3]

When the angel announced that Zechariah and Elizabeth were going to have son, he told Zechariah "you are to call him John" (Lk. 1:13). This name means *God is gracious*.[4]

The birth of John was foretold by the prophet Isaiah:

---

[1] Ann Spangler, Jean E. Syswerda, *Women of the Bible: A One-Year Devotional Study of Women in Scripture* (Zondervan, 2007), 283

[2] Margaret Feinberg, *Spark Your Joy: A 4-Week Advent Bible Study Devotional* (Margaret Feinberg, 2014), 8

[3] Jazmin N. Frank, *Women of the Covenant: Discovering God's Faithfulness to Women in a Broken and Hurting World* (Beautifully Devoted Resources, 2021), 18-21, 25-27

[4] Feinberg, *Spark Your Joy*, 8

"A voice of one crying out:
Prepare the way of the Lord in the wilderness;
make a straight highway for our God in the desert.
Every valley will be lifted up,
and every mountain and hill will be leveled;
the uneven ground will become smooth
and the rough places, a plain.
And the glory of the Lord will appear,
and all humanity together will see it,
for the mouth of the Lord has spoken."
Isaiah 40:3-5, CSB[5]

Now here are Elizabeth—*God is my oath*—and Zechariah—
God remembers—after hundreds of years without a prophet
speaking God's Word to Israel,[6] seeing that promise unfold in their
lives, through their lives.

The grace of God coming to them in their son, and coming for
each and every person in *His Son*.

—

When the angel told Zechariah he and Elizabeth would have a
child, Zechariah doubted this promise because of their old age, and
because of this doubt, he was made mute until the baby was born
(Lk. 1:18-20).

After their relatives argued against Elizabeth naming their
newborn son John, Zechariah wrote for all to see, "His name is
John" (Lk. 1:63), the name the Lord had chosen for this child.
Immediately, Zechariah regained his voice "and he began to speak,
praising God" (Lk. 1:64) And at some point, he "was filled with
the Holy Spirit and prophesied" (Lk. 1:67).

We read this prophecy in Luke 1:67-79, a passage some Bible
translations title "Zachariah's Song."[7]

---

[5] See also John 1:23

[6] *What were Isreal's 400 years of silence?* Got Questions Ministries, 2016, http://
www.compellingtruth.org/400-years-of-silence.html

[7] Such as the *New International Version* (copyright 1973, 1978, 1984, 2011 by
Biblica, Inc.)

Based on this order of events, it makes sense Zechariah would be praising and thanking God. Of course he's thankful and worshipful—his prayers have finally been answered!

But we're still here. Still waiting, still praying, still dreaming. Still single.

While Zechariah's praise was in response to answered prayer, it was coming from heart that already worshiped the Lord (Lk. 1:5-6).

When I read this song of praise and prophesy, I hear echoes of themes and language from the Old Testament Scriptures, which Zechariah would have learned, studied, memorized, and recited his whole life. Elizabeth too would have been familiar with them. These were words the nation of Israel had declared and sung and confessed for generations to remember God's faithfulness to His covenant through the generations.

Zechariah and Elizabeth recognized this gift of a child was just more of God's faithfulness upon faithfulness, grace upon grace, blessing upon blessing, from generation to generation.

We may still be in a place of *still-ness*, but what if in the midst of the disappointment we're feeling, we took some time to remember, reflect on, and rejoice in the ways God has shown Himself faithful in this past year? What if we were to look back and look for the ways God was weaving His goodness and grace in us, around us, and through us?

Even if it doesn't look like prayers being answered as hoped or dreams coming true as desired or milestones being reached as expected, that doesn't mean God wasn't there, wasn't working, wasn't faithfully unfolding His promises in our lives.

—

So many of the stories in Scripture are about people in a place of *still-ness*. This story of Zechariah and Elizabeth is just one of them.

Abraham and Sarah were given a promise of offspring numerous as the stars in the sky, then they waited into old age before having a child (Gen. 11:1-3, 15:1-5, 21:1-7).

Joseph had a dream of his brothers bowing down to him, then he suffered through betrayal and unjust treatment before seeing that dream become a reality and God turning what was meant for harm into good (Gen. 37:5-36, 39:1-20, 42:6-9, 45:1-28).

Jochebed placed Moses in a reed basket, then remained in slavery. And based on Moses being 80 years-old when he led the Israelites out of Egypt, it's likely Jochebed didn't live to see Israel set free (Ex. 2:1-4, Ex. 7:7).

David was anointed king by the prophet Samual, then endured through King Saul's attempts to kill him before coming to the throne (1 Sam. 16:1-13, 18:8-11, 19:1-24; 2 Sam. 2:1-4).

God's people were given promise after promise that the Messiah would come, then experienced 400 years of His silence[8] before an angel appeared to a young woman and told her she would bear the Promised One (Lk. 1:26-38).

We can read these stories in full, and see in them God's perfect timing and plan at work to bring about the redemption and restoration of His beloved creation.

He is doing the same in our own *still-ness*. We can look back on these Bible stories and see how God was writing His Gospel story all along. How wonderful will it be to look back on our own stories and see the same!

Disappointment doesn't have to be the defining narrative of our stories, our Christmas season, or our singleness.

The story of God's faithfulness to deliver, comfort, heal, restore, provide, and bless—it's our story, too!

And like Elizabeth, whether or not all our dreams come true just as we had hoped and desired, we'll be able to look back on our story, our year, our singleness, and say: *The Lord has done this for me* (Lk. 1:25, CSB).

---

[8] *What were Isreal's 400 years of silence?* http://www.compellingtruth.org/400-years-of-silence.html

Read Luke 1:67-79

What are some of the things Zechariah praises God for in this passage?

Think back on the past year: where do you see God's faithfulness? What has He done for you? What can you praise Him for?

Dear Faithful God, I thank You for these ways You've shown Yourself faithful and good in this past year: _____. In the places of still-ness, I'm trusting that You are still working for my good and Your glory, even when I don't see it. I love You and praise You. Amen.

Chapter 4
The Lord Remembered Her

At the end of each year, I take some time to reflect on the past year and then set goals for the next.

A few years ago, as Christmas approached and I pondered what goals I might set for the new year, one area I knew I wanted to grow in was in prayer. I sensed a stirring in my spirit that I needed to have a regular and intentional prayer time each day, not just praying when I needed or wanted something.

That very Christmas, my siblings gifted me a book called *Praying with Jane,* a devotional that explores and draws encouragement from prayers Jane Austen wrote, and included at the end of each chapter was a prayer prompt for one's own prayers.[1]

My siblings didn't know about my desire and decision to cultivate prayer in my life. They just know that I'm a follower of Jesus and a fan of Jane Austen, so of course such a book seemed like a good gift!

This book was not only a thoughtful gift from my siblings, but an encouraging confirmation from my Heavenly Father.

In being given this pink-and-teal-covered devotional for Christmas, God was showing me that He already saw my heart, was already responding to my prayers, and was already working His grace and goodness in my obedience.

In that moment, I felt seen and known.

------

[1] Rachel Dodges, *Praying with Jane: 31 Days Through the Prayers of Jane Austen* (Bethany House Publishers, 2018)

—

One of my favorite stories in the Bible is the story of Hannah. It's one of my favorites not only because I relate to Hannah, but also because there is truth and encouragement in her story for us during those moments when we *don't* feel seen or known; when instead we feel overlooked, left out, and forgotten.

We read Hannah's story in 1 Samuel 1-2. And while it's not a Christmas story, it does take place during an event that happened annually in the life of Hannah: each year, she would travel with her husband Elkanah, his other wife Peninnah, and Elkanah and Peninnah's children to Shiloh, for an annual time of offering sacrifices and worshipping (1 Sam. 1:3).

Unlike Peninnah, Hannah didn't have any children; like so many other women in Scripture, she was barren (1 Sam. 1:5).

I don't know if her barrenness felt more empty, if her longing for a child pressed more insistently, if her sorrow ached more tenderly during this yearly pilgrimage compared to her every day life, but it certainly didn't lighten or lessen during this time for Hannah.

And it didn't help that during this time especially, Peninnah chose to "taunt Hannah and make fun of her because the Lord had kept her from having children. Year after year it was the same— Peninnah would taunt Hannah as they went to the Tabernacle. Each time, Hannah would be reduced to tears and would not even eat" (1 Sam. 1:6-7).

Hannah's husband Elkanah would always give her a double portion of the sacrificial meat "because he loved her" (1 Sam. 1:5) and would try to lift her spirits by making light of her longings: "'Why are you crying, Hannah?' Elkanah would ask. 'Why aren't you eating? Why be downhearted just because you have no children? You have me—isn't that better than having ten sons?'" (1 Sam. 1:8)

And when the priest Eli saw Hannah pouring out the longings of her heart in prayer, he was quick to jump to conclusions and give a solution: "As she was praying to the Lord, Eli watched her. Seeing her lips moving but hearing no sound, he thought she had been drinking. 'Must you come here drunk?' he demanded. 'Throw away your wine!'" (1 Sam. 1:12-14)

As single people, when those yearly holiday gatherings come around, we can experience similar responses to our singleness as Hannah did to her childlessness:

There are those who make comments and ask questions and even poke fun about our lack of a romantic partner that, whether by intention, because of insensitivity, or because of ignorance, are hurtful to us.

There are those who in their desire for us to be happy and enjoy the season can end up making light of the hard stuff of singleness.

And there are those who are quick to offer advice about our singleness without first listening to what's in our heart.

We often come to the holiday season with a mixed bag from the year: joys and sorrows; victories and regrets; gratitude and disappointment; successes and mistakes; adventures we're so glad we experienced and pain we wish to never experienced again; burdens and blessings; prayers answered and prayers unanswered; hopes and fears; lessons learned and things we're still trying to figure out.

Even though this is a book for singles, even as you may come to the Christmas season with your singleness feeling extra *single*, there is more to your life, more to *you*, than your single status.

Yet in the many emotions we're experiencing, in the hardships we're going through, even in the good things we're celebrating, we can feel unseen, unknown, and alone.

Yeah, I can definitely relate to Hannah.

But like I said, there's more than just relating to her. There is also encouragement to be found in how *God* responded to her.

—

In 1 Samuel 1:9-19, we read of a particular time Hannah traveled with Elkanah and his other family to Shiloh. After they had finished the sacrificial meal, "Hannah got up and went to pray" (v. 9, NLT). She was "in deep anguish, crying bitterly as she prayed to the Lord." (v. 10, NLT)

While the ways Peninah, Elkaneh, and Eli responded to Hannah's longings, sorrow, and heartache weren't always compassionate, helpful, or encouraging, here's how God responded to her:

"Early the next morning they arose and worshiped before the Lord and then went back to their home at Ramah. Elkanah made love to his wife Hannah, and the Lord remembered her. So in the course of time Hannah became pregnant and gave birth to a son. She named him Samuel, saying, 'Because I asked the Lord for him.'" 1 Samuel 1:19-20

The Lord remembered her.

When the Bible talks about God remembering something, it's not saying He forgot, and then something jogged His memory and caused Him to remember again. God didn't forget about Hannah, only to remember her existence and needs and longings and hopes when she cried out to Him in prayer.

The word "remembered" in this verse (and throughout the Old Testament) comes from the Hebrew word *zakar*. This word speaks of remembering in such a way as to *never* forget. It means to mark or record, to retain in thought, to be mindful and to think on.[2]

Zakar is the word used when Scripture speaks of God remembering His eternal covenant with His people, and so moving to act on their behalf.[3]

We see this in Exodus 2:24 as God hears the cries of His people in slavery in Egypt:

"God heard their groaning and he remembered his covenant with Abraham, with Isaac and with Jacob. So God looked on the Israelites and was concerned about them."

Zakar here marks a turning point in the story, because in the very next chapter, God speaks to Moses from a burning bush, calling him to lead His people to freedom.

We also see this word used in a similar way to 1 Samuel 1:19 in Genesis 30:22, when Rachel, another woman who suffered from infertility, is *remembered* by God and then conceives a child.

Zakar is used to convey the truth that God doesn't forget His people or His promises. He didn't forget Noah or those with him in the ark (Gen. 8:1). He didn't forget the Israelites during 400 years of slavery (Ex. 2:24). He didn't forget His people as they wandered

---

[2] James Strong, *The New Strong's Expanded Exhaustive Concordance of the Bible* (Thomas Nelson Publishers, 2010), 74-75

[3] Strong, *The New Strong's Expanded Exhaustive Concordance of the Bible*, 74-75

through desert wilderness (Ps. 105:40-42). He didn't forget His people when they were facing enemies in battle (Num. 10:9). He didn't forget His covenant with His people even as time after time, they did (Ps. 78:10-72). He didn't forget Rachel or Hannah in their waiting and longing and aching (Gen. 30:22; 1 Sam. 1:19).

—

In that simple phrase "the Lord remembered her", we see God's heart for us who may feel overlooked in the midst of all we're carrying and feeling and experiencing and navigating and desiring and celebrating.

God remembered Hannah, and His plan for her life included answering her prayers for a child.

Your prayers may not be answered in ways you expect; your dreams may not be fulfilled in ways you imagine; your longings may not be met in ways you had hoped.

But God *will* answer.

Because He *remembers* you. You are recorded in His heart and retained in His thoughts.

He remembers you when the questions about your singleness and lack of questions about your daily life cause you to feel overlooked. He remembers you as you navigate all the holiday to-dos and family dynamics solo. He remembers you in your hopes to share the wins with someone who will celebrate, and in your longings to have a second shoulder under the burdens with you.

And His remembering moves Him to act.

So He is also *with* you in it all. Present in the loneliness. Comforting in the sorrow. Listening to your heart's cry. Guiding through the messy and difficult. Providing in the needs and longings. Working His grace and goodness in and through you. Delighting in you and rejoicing over you.

Loving you, *always*.

Read 1 Samuel 1:21-2:10

Like Zachariah, Hannah responds to her answered prayers for a child with a song of praise. In her song, what words are used to describe God, His heart toward us, and His actions for us?

What prayers do you need to trust God is hearing? What areas of your life do you need to trust God is seeing?

When was a time you felt seen, known, and loved—by God and by others?

Dear Heavenly Father, thank You for always hearing my prayers and seeing my heart. Right now, an area where I feel unseen and overlooked is _____. Please meet me here. Thank You for never forgetting me, for always remembering me, and for fully knowing and loving me. I love You and praise You. Amen.

Chapter 5
The God Who is With Us

It was my first Christmas living by myself, and I thought I might have to spend it by myself.

In the days leading up to Christmas, I got really sick; my whole body ached, my nose was simultaneously runny and stuffed up, my ears were plugged, and my throat was the most sore it's ever been.

After multiple days of these symptoms, I went to the hospital, got tested for strep throat and many other things, and all those tests came back negative. "You just have a really bad cold," the doctor told me.

So I went back to my small apartment, continued to rest, take medicine, drink warm water with honey, and eat a lot of soup.

Not only did I feel unwell physically, I also felt very anxious. Because the dishes were piling up. There were still gifts to wrap. I needed to do laundry. My fridge and cupboards were getting emptier by the day. There were certain foods I had said I would make for the Christmas gatherings that I knew I wasn't going to be able to make. I ran out of soup. And then I ran out of medicine.

Each day I was sick, the to-do list grew longer—the to-do list that gets checked off by me and me alone.

And on top of it all, I didn't know if I'd be well enough to go to the Christmas gatherings with my family. Would I spend Christmas alone, with only the to-dos I hadn't gotten done?

It was definitely one of those instances when being single felt extra *single*.

You may not be laid up with sickness this holiday season, but there may be added to-dos and responsibilities, plans to make and preparations to complete, hard decisions and difficult family dynamics, or some other burden you're shouldering on your own that's causing you to feel stressed and weary in this season.

Christmas is a celebration of Jesus' birth, and when His birth was first announced by a host of heavenly angels to group of lowly shepherds, it was proclaimed as "good tidings of great joy which will be to all people... And on earth peace, goodwill toward men!" (Lk. 2:10, 14, NKJV)

But what about some peace for our stressed minds, some joy for our weary hearts? What do we do when we're tired of doing it all alone?

—

If we were sitting across from one another and you shared your anxiousness, weariness, and stressed-out-ness with me, I wouldn't jump to giving advice to fix it. I wouldn't diminish what you're feeling in an effort to help you feel better. I wouldn't downplay what's hard about singleness in an effort to help you see the good.

I'd say, *I understand.*

I'd say, *I get it.*

I'd say, *That is hard.*

Because I've been there myself, many times.

And I'd hope you'd feel seen. I'd hope you'd feel unashamed in how you're feeling and safe to cry if you needed. I'd hope you'd have space to breathe deep and just be.

You and I aren't physically sitting with one another—though I hope this book gives you sense of solidarity and that I'm with you in spirit! But there is Someone who is always present with you: *Immanuel, God with us.*

I don't say that as a platitude. I don't say that to sweep your weariness and loneliness under the rug.

Because God doesn't. He isn't aloof to the burdens you're carrying; He isn't indifferent to your worn-out heart; He isn't annoyed by or uncomfortable with the tears your stress and anxiousness cause to spill out of you.

We've talked quite a bit about that name *Immanuel*, about this truth of *God with us.* 2 chapters after Isaiah prophesied that the Child born of a virgin would be called by this name (Is. 7:14), he

33

prophesied again about this Child and other names by which He would be called:

> *"For a child is born to us,*
> *a son is given to us.*
> *The government will rest on his shoulders.*
> *And he will be called:*
> *Wonderful Counselor, Mighty God,*
> *Everlasting Father, Prince of Peace.*
> *His government and its peace*
> *will never end.*
> *He will rule with fairness and justice from the throne of his*
> *ancestor David*
> *for all eternity.*
> *The passionate commitment of the Lord of Heaven's Armies*
> *will make this happen!" Isaiah 9:6-7, NLT*

The names of God we read in Scripture are not just titles by which He is to be called. Rather, they are a revelation of *who He is*. God's name describes His character.[1] It speaks of how He relates to and interacts with His creation, with us.

Wonderful Counselor, Mighty God, Everlasting Father, Prince of Peace: this is how the God who is with us is described; this is *who* the God who is with us *is*.

So let's take closer look at these names and what they mean—how God reveals Himself to us through them, and how knowing *who* the God who is with us *is* can bring peace to our stressed minds and joy to our weary hearts:

Wonderful Counselor

God is wise and He gives wisdom to His people.

We see this in the Old Testament, as He gives His law and sends prophets to declare His Word. And in the New Testament, He writes His law of wisdom and goodness on our hearts through giving His Holy Spirit (Jer. 31:33; Rom. 8:4).

In John 14:16-18, when Jesus promises to send the Holy Spirit to His disciples, the word He uses for the Spirit is the Greek word *parakletos*. Depending on which Bible translation you read, the

---

[1] Kay Arthur, *Lord, I Want to Know You* (Multnomah Books, 1992), 15

English word used could be Counselor, Advocate, or Helper.[2] "Comforter", "strength giver", "friend", "revealer", and "mediator" are more words (among others) this single word *parakletos* could be translated to.[3]

All these words speak of the work the Holy Spirit does in our hearts and lives—how He guides us in truth, supports and strengthens us to walk in obedience, and comforts and encourages us in sorrow and hardship (Jn. 16:13; Rom. 8:1-17; Jn. 14:26-27).

When we're facing hard and heavy and heartbreaking stuff in our lives, we are not alone. We have a Wonderful Counselor who is not only with us, but *living in us* (Jn. 14:17), comforting our hearts, strengthening our spirits, and giving wisdom to our minds.

Mighty God

Our God is sovereign and all-powerful, able to accomplish His purpose and will.

The things that for us feel too hard to bear, too heavy to carry, too overwhelming to navigate, are not too much for the Lord Almighty!

A virgin conceiving a child (Matt. 1:18), the blind seeing (Lk. 18:35-43), a sea parting into a dry path Ex. 14:21-22), five loaves and two fish becoming enough to feed 5,000 (Matt. 14:15-21), the deaf hearing (Mk. 7:32-35), demons fleeing (Mk. 1:34), the dead being raised to life (Jn. 11:1-44), all impossible, and yet "with God all things are possible" (Matt. 19:26).

The same Mighty God who accomplished all this is with us!

Everlasting Father

In this name, we see God's heart for us: that of a Father who loves, cares for, and delights in His children (1 Jn. 3:1; Matt. 6:25-24; Eph. 1:4-6).

It is because He is our Father that we can "approach [His] throne of grace with boldness, so that we may receive mercy and find grace to help us in time of need" (Heb. 4:16, CSB); that we can "cast all [our] anxiety on him because he cares for [us]" (1 Pet. 5:7); that we can "not be anxious about anything, but in every

---

[2] *Christian Standard Bible* (copyright 2017 by Holman Bible Publishers), *New Living Translation* (copyright 1996, 2004, 2015 by Tyndale House Foundation), *New King James Version* (copyright 1982 by Thomas Nelson), respectively.

[3] Frank More, *The Holy Spirit* (The Foundry Publishing, 2023), 120

situation, by prayer and petition, with thanksgiving, present [our] requests to God" (Phil. 4:7).

Because as our Father, God is not aloof to our burdens, indifferent to our heartache, or annoyed by our needs.

He *desires* a relationship with us, His beloved children—a relationship in which we are so assured of His love for us that we wholeheartedly trust in His care for us, knowing we are safe and secure in His embrace.

Prince of Peace

Through His death and resurrection, Jesus makes the way for us who were separated from God to be reconciled to God. And in this relationship, He makes the way for us to participate in the restoration of creation to the Father's design of *shalom*: all creation being whole, healthy, and harmonious in all relationships.[4]

Our peace isn't found in all the to-dos being checked off the list, in a full bank account, in having a romantic partner by our side, in every area of our lives being smooth and stable and secure, in things going according to our plans and expectations. Our peace in found in Christ—in knowing He is in control and cares for us, and in submitting to His care and control.

The verses preceding these names of Jesus in Isaiah 9 give a picture of the peace He would bring: freedom from laborious striving; rescue from oppression; a lifting of burdens; light driving away darkness, fear, and despair; unity between Jews and Gentiles; a ceasing of conflict; having provision and abundance for all needs (vv. 1-5).

This peace would be found in the Child born to us, called Wonderful Counselor, Mighty God, Everlasting Father, Prince of Peace.

He is the One who is seated on the throne, who is sovereign over all, and to His reign there will be no end (v. 7).

—

We can have peace and joy because of who God is. And He is *with us*.

---

[4] H. Ray Dunning, *Reflecting the Divine Image: Christian Ethics in Wesleyan Perspective* (Wipf and Stock Publishers, 1998), 47

But sometimes, He doesn't feel near. Sometimes, the weariness, stress, and worry make it hard to sense His presence. What then?

If you and I were sitting together, and you had space to cry and breathe and just be, and you then wanted some advice for leaning into these truths of who God is and that He is with us, here's what I'd offer:

Remember God's Character

In the midst of stress, worry, and overwhelm, there's a description of God I find myself recalling again and again:

> *The Lord is my shepherd;*
> *I shall not want. Psalm 23:1, NKJV*

Remembering this Psalm helps me remember who God is: my Good Shepherd—my perfect, loving, mighty, caring, wise, only-does-what-is-for-my-best Shepherd.

And in remembering who He is, I remember that in Him *I lack nothing; I have all that I need* (Ps. 23:1 in the NIV and NLT, respectively).

Perhaps there's a different Bible verse that resonates with you and helps you remember who God is. Or maybe there's a song that lifts your heart and lifts your eyes to refocus on Jesus. Or perhaps whispering a prayer, or gazing upon God's creation, or simply taking a moment to be still and notice His nearness are practices that help (or could help) you remember and meditate on His character.

Ask for What You Need

That week I was so sick, when I found myself in need of more medicine and more soup, I texted my parents and asked them to bring me some. And they did.

I texted my friends and asked them to pray for healing in my body and peace in my heart. And they did.

I prayed and asked God to give me rest and peace amidst the anxiety I was experiencing. And He did.

As lonely as doing the to-dos, carrying the burdens, making the decisions in our singleness can feel, we don't have to it alone. We can ask for what we need, from God and from others.

In Philippians 4:7, we're invited to present our requests to God —to ask Him for the comfort, hope, peace, joy, wisdom, help, whatever it is we need—trusting He will "meet all [our] needs according to His glorious riches in Christ Jesus" (Phil. 4:19).

Asking others for help can be a bit harder for some of us, because we don't want to appear "needy"; because we may not know who to ask; because we're afraid (or assuming) we'll be told no; because there have been times when no one showed up for us.

But in Galatians 6:2, we are called to "carry each other's burdens." We can't do this if we don't share our burdens and make known the support, encouragement, and help we need.

And needing help isn't being a burden; it's being open to being loved right where you are.

Invite Others In

Sometimes, the thing we need isn't soup or medicine or someone to take out the trash.

The thing we need is a listening ear, a shoulder to cry on, an embrace.

The thing we need is *presence*. Someone to just be with us, and with whom we can just be.

Are there others we can invite into the weariness and loneliness we're experiencing, with whom we can share where we're at and what's on our hearts, to be present together in support and solidarity?

Yes, it means being vulnerable, and by definition, vulnerability is a risk. But vulnerability can also create relationships of safety, strength, and compassion. Because there are many others who are also weary and lonely (and not just other single people). There are many who would respond, *I understand, I get it, that is hard*, and then give you a hug.

Leave Room for Rest

Doing the to-dos alone, the added hustle and bustle of the holidays, the heavy emotions we may be experiencing during this season, navigating singleness (especially when we've been single longer than we had hoped)—no wonder we feel weary!

In Matthew 11:28, Jesus invites us:

"Come to me, all you who are weary and burdened, and I will give you rest."

We need to leave room for rest. We need to leave room for sitting in Jesus' presence. We need to leave room for being filled with *His* strength, *His* peace, *His* joy, *His* wisdom.

If you're anything like me, this mean resisting the fear of disappointing others and our need to people-please, and saying "no" to the things you don't really have the time, energy, or finances for.

This could also mean saying "yes" to things you normally don't prioritize but that fill you up, whether that's going for a walk, getting coffee with a friend, or creating something just because.

—

These practices I share aren't meant to be a quick fix for the weariness and loneliness you're experiencing.

They are meant to help you breathe and just be, knowing you are held in the weariness, known in the loneliness, and loved in your singleness by the God who is with us.

(And in case you're wondering: I did get better in time to go to the Christmas gatherings, though I did lose my voice for several days!)

Read Isaiah 9:1-7

How is Jesus' reign described in this passage?

Wonderful Counselor, Mighty God, Everlasting Father, Prince of Peace: which of these names resonates most with you right now? What name do you need to remember is who God is?

On pages 37-39 are some ideas of ways we can lean into the truth of who God is when we're stressed and worried. Which one do you want to practice this holiday season?

Dear God, I praise You for who You are: Wonderful Counselor, Mighty God, Everlasting Father, Prince of Peace. Right now, I am stressed and worried about _____. I ask You for _____. I cast these worries onto You and trust You will provide all I need. I love You and praise You. Amen.

Chapter 6
Why Them but Not Me?

For many of us, the holidays are a time of gathering together with family. The gatherings may be small or large; near or far; all-day parties or evening dinners; quiet and laid-back or loud and bustling; or some combination of it all.

Each year for Christmas, I have three family gatherings I go to: one at my paternal grandparents' house, where it's common for there to be around 30 people; one at my maternal grandparents' house, where there's less people but just as much activity; and one at my parents' house with my immediate family, where I feel most at home.

Except for my three cousins who are under 16 years-old, I'm the only one out of all my siblings and cousins who's never brought a significant other to any of the family gatherings, who's never *had* a significant other to bring.

When we're gathering together for the holidays, and each holiday season another sibling, another cousin, another friend, is bringing a significant other, is engaged, is married, is having kids —this can stir up some feelings in us who are *not*.

It can stir up sadness, disappointment, confusion, and so many other emotions as we see others getting the thing we've been longing for, hoping for, praying for... but we're still single.

It can also stir up comparison, envy, and even resentment towards others in their happiness, because this happiness that's happening for them isn't happening for us too, as much as we may desire it.

As the cousins, siblings, and friends share their happy news of romance and marriage and growing families, we want to be happy for them, joining in the congratulations and celebrations. But even as we smile and well-wish, there's a pang in our hearts and we wonder, *Why them but not me?*

Many of us know the Bible tells us to not envy (Gal. 5:26). But when all the family is gathered together, and the cousin or sibling or friend makes their happy announcement, what then? How do we not become envious when our hearts are aching with longing for a romance, a marriage, a baby of our own? How do we be happy for them and with them while all these other feelings are roiling inside us?

—

Many of us know the Bible tells us to not envy, but what does the Bible tell us about *how* to not envy?

In Galatians 5, the apostle Paul (who, by the way, was single) lists envy as one of the acts of the sinful nature (vv. 19-21). He says, "The sinful nature wants to do evil, which is just the opposite of what the Spirit wants" (v. 17, NLT).

It can feel impossible to not compare ourselves to others and become envious of them when all these longings and emotions are flooding our hearts. And in the sinful nature, which desires only to please self regardless of God's will or others' needs, it is impossible (Rom. 7:18-24, 8:5-8).

But we have been given a new nature, one that is being cultivated and refined in us:

"Therefore, if anyone is in Christ, he is a new creation; the old has passed away, and see, the new has come!" 2 Corinthians 5:17, CSB

"Put on your new nature, created to be like God—truly righteous and holy." Ephesians 4:24, NLT

"And the Lord—who is the Spirit—makes us more and more like him as we are changed into his glorious image." 2 Corinthians 3:18, NLT

This new nature is not self-seeking; it is not powerless to resist temptation; it is not rebellious to God's goodness and wisdom; it is not indifferent to the well-being of others. This new nature is *Christ-likeness*, created and cultivated and refined in us by the *very Spirit of Christ in us*.

During His last meal with His disciples, Jesus gave this promise:

*"I will ask the Father, and he will give you another advocate to help you and be with you forever—the Spirit of truth. The world cannot accept him, because it neither sees him nor knows him. But you know him, for he lives with you and **will be in you**. I will not leave you as orphans; I will come to you." John 14:16-18, emphasis mine.*

Our Immanuel God is not only *with us*, but *in us* through the presence of His Spirit. This is the nearest closeness, the deepest intimacy, the most *withness* there is: God Himself dwelling in us to unite us with Him in love and desire, to confirm we are His sons and daughters, to seal us for eternity with Him, and to give us confident assurance of His love for us and our eternal salvation in Him (Rom. 5:5, 8:16; Gal. 5:16-17; Eph. 1:13-14).

In other places in the New Testament, the Holy Spirit is called the Spirit of God's Son (Gal. 4:6), the Spirit of wisdom and revelation (Eph. 1:17), the Spirit who raised Jesus from the grave (Rom. 8:11). The Holy Spirit, who unites, confirms, seals, and assures, also transforms us to be more and more like Christ (2 Cor. 3:18). He teaches and empowers us to live more and more as the holy and dearly loved children of God that we are (Col. 3:12). He guides and helps us to walk more and more in the way of love and reflect our Father's love (Eph. 5:1-2).

We may feel like we can't help but envy. I know that feeling. Even as we try, we feel powerless to stop the spiral of *Why them but not me?*, to halt the envy we sense taking root, to change the attitude that's turned sour towards another's happiness.

In Galatians 5, when Paul speaks of the sinful nature and the Holy Spirit, he speaks of them as polar opposites. This means that while in the sinful nature we "cannot do the good we want to do" (Rom. 7:19), there is a flip side: when we walk by the Spirit, we won't gratify or give into the desires of the sinful nature (Gal. 5:16)!

So when we're gathered with family and friends and one of them shares their news and smiles their happiness, and we sense envy (or any other un-Christ-like attitude) trying to take root in us, what does it mean for us to "walk by the Spirit"?

—

There's a lot that could be said on the subject of walking by the Spirit; whole books have been written on this topic. But for this chapter, and for those times when comparison, envy, resentment, or other un-Christ-like attitudes start to stir in us upon hearing someone else's good news, we're going to focus on a few foundational principles of walking by the Spirit: *confession*, *repentance*, and *obedience*.

Confession

One of the ways the Holy Spirit works in us is through convicting us of sin. When there is an attitude, an action, a thought-pattern, a habit, a way we've spoken to or treated someone else that are not aligned with Christ's character and the Father's will, the Spirit will convict our spirits of this.

Conviction is often not a pleasant experience, because it usually means confronting and confessing the ugliness of our sin and the harm it has done to others, to ourselves, and to our intimacy with God.

But conviction is a grace from God, because He convicts us of sin so that we may confess our sin; we may recognize and acknowledge our brokenness and waywardness, our need for healing and correction, and that wholeness and righteousness are created and cultivated in us through Christ alone (Rom. 3:20-26; Tit. 2:11-14).

When we sense those envious feelings stirring in us, we walk by the Spirit by responding to His conviction with *confession*, confessing the envy and asking God to "forgive us our sins and purify us of all unrighteousness," which He will be faithful to do (1 Jn. 1:9).

Repentance

Confession and repentance go hand-in-hand, because "godly sorrow brings repentance" (2 Cor. 7:10). The Holy Spirit doesn't convict us of sin just to make us aware of it, but to invite us to "[strip] off your old sinful nature and all its wicked deeds" and to "put on your new nature, and be renewed as you learn to know your Creator and become like him" (Col. 3:9-10, NLT).

Repentance is consciously and actively turning away from sin —the actions, attitudes, thought-patterns, habits of the old sinful nature—and turning towards Jesus for salvation and transformation (Acts 3:19; 1 Pet. 2:24-25).

As we confess and ask forgiveness for envy, we continue walking by the Spirit by asking God to remove the envy from our hearts and change our attitudes towards others to be more and more aligned with His love, compassion, and grace for them.

Another component of repentance from sin is accountability. James 5:16 says, "Confess your sins to each other and pray for each other so that you may be healed" (NLT) and Hebrews 10:24 says, "Let us consider how to stir up one another toward love and good works" (ESV).

We're not meant to grow in Christ-likeness alone. We need to have trusted people in our lives with whom we can share the things we're struggling with (including sinful actions, thoughts, and attitudes), the ways the Holy Spirit is convicting and working in us, and the victories we're experiencing in Christ. We need trusted people who will check-in with us, celebrate with us, and hold us accountable to walking by the Spirit, not to shame us for not being "good enough", but to encourage and support us in following Jesus and growing in His likeness.

Obedience

The change from the old nature of sin to the new nature of Christ-likeness isn't something we accomplish by our own willpower.

In Ephesians 1:19-20, Paul writes to the church:

"I also pray that you will understand the incredible greatness of God's power for us who believe in him. This is the same mighty power that raised Christ from the dead and seated him in the place of honor at God's right hand in the heavenly realms." NLT

And in another letter, Paul writes:

"The power of the life-giving Spirit has freed you from the power of sin that leads to death... The Spirit of God, who raised

Jesus from the dead, lives in you... Therefore, dear brothers and sisters, you have no obligation to do what your sinful nature urges you to do. For if you live by its dictates, you will die. But if through the power of Spirit you put to death the deeds of your sinful nature, you will live." Romans 8:2, 11-13, NLT

It is through His Holy Spirit in us that God gives us not only the desire but also the power to act and think and speak and *be* in a new way: *His* way (Phil. 2:13).

This isn't to say we sit passive. We are to *walk* by the Spirit, and we keep in step with Him by submitting to and participating in the work He wants to do in and through us:

"His divine power has given us everything we need for a godly life through our knowledge of him who called us by his own glory and goodness. Through these he has given us his very great and precious promises, so that through them you may participate in the divine nature, having escaped the corruption in the world caused by evil desires.

"For this very reason, make every effort to add to your faith goodness; and to goodness, knowledge; and to knowledge self-control; and to self-control, perseverance; and to perseverance, godliness; and to godliness, mutual affection; and to mutual affection, love. For if you possess these qualities in increasing measure, they will keep you from being ineffective and unproductive in your knowledge of our Lord Jesus Christ." 2 Peter 1:3-8

As we confess and repent of un-Christ-likeness, there will be things the Holy Spirit prompts us to do to "put to death the sinful, earthly things lurking within you" (Col. 3:5) and to "participate in the divine nature" (2 Pet. 1:4)—the new nature of Christ-likeness He has created and is cultivating in us.

He may prompt you to practice gratitude to replace the thoughts of comparison; to forgive those you've had ill-feelings towards; to offer to help and serve others in both their need and their celebration; to pray for someone you've felt resentment toward; to stop certain media consumption because of the envy it stirs inside you; or something else! Whatever the Holy Spirit leads us to do, "let us follow the Spirit's leading in every part of our lives" (Gal. 5:25, NLT).

—

In Galatians 5, envy is listed among the acts of the sinful nature, but just a few verses later, we read a description of the new nature the Holy Spirit creates and cultivates in us:

"But the Holy Spirit produces this kind of fruit in our lives: love, joy, peace, patience, kindness, goodness, faithfulness, gentleness, and self-control." Galatians 5:22-23, NLT

This sounds like the sort of heart-posture I want to have in my singleness. This sounds like the sort of attitude I want to have towards others. This sounds like the sort of person I want to *be*, not just on the good days, but every day.

We are promised that as we walk by the Spirit, He will create, cultivate, and bear forth this fruit in our lives. He will uproot the old ways of the sinful nature and grow us in Christ-likeness.

As the holidays approach, let's take some time to confess any proneness to be envious of others; let's ask God to give us a new heart posture that's aligned with His heart; let's submit to the Spirit as He grows compassion, joy, peace, and other Christ-like character in us. And as the holidays arrive, and then pass, let's continue to do so!

The work God does in us to grow us in Christ-likeness is often not through the flip of a switch, an overnight miracle, a one-and-done gift.

It's often through slow (sometimes painfully slow) and steady growth, as He teaches and guides, prunes and shapes, convicts and forgives, provides and empowers.

I don't think it's a coincidence that this Christ-like nature we are called to put on is likened to fruit: that which is to be tended and nurtured and cultivated, day by day and season by season.

And the Father is called the Gardener (Jn. 15:1): the One who personally tends to and cares for our growth with a tenacious and indefatigable love.

And Jesus is called the Vine (Jn. 15:5): the One who gives His own life to be our Life-Source, in whom we find nourishment and rest.

And the Holy Spirit is called the Advocate (Jn. 14:16): the One who dwells in us, confirming Whose and who we are, rooting truth into our hearts and minds, so our very nature is transformed, and we want not what the sinful nature craves, but what the Spirit desires, and as we walk with Him we are empowered to bear not the rot of sin and death, but the fruit of light and life.

Read Romans 8:1-17

In this passage, what contrasts do you see between living according to the sinful nature (or the flesh) and living according to the Spirit?

How has the Holy Spirit grown and cultivated Christ-likeness in you this past year?

Are there any areas in your life the Holy Spirit is inviting you to confess, repent of, and/or be obedient to Him in?

Dear Heavenly Father, thank You for the gift of Your Holy Spirit, to live in me and help me live as Your child. I confess _____. Please uproot this sin and grow in me the fruit of _____. I love You and praise You. Amen.

Chapter 7

Reach Out

You know how sometimes in the Bible, there are those verses containing minute details that are easily overlooked and passed by? For a long time, Luke 1:56 was one such verse for me:

"Mary stayed with Elizabeth for about three months and then returned home."

After an angel came to Mary and told her she would bear the Son of God even though she was a virgin (Lk. 1:26-38), Mary "hurried to a town in the hill country of Judea, where she entered Zechariah's home and greeted Elizabeth" (Lk. 1:39-40), who we know was also pregnant, even though she was past child-bearing age and said to be barren.

Upon hearing the words "You have found favor with God. The Holy Spirit will come upon you and the power of the Most High will overshadow you. So the Holy One to be born will be called the Son of God" (Lk. 1:30, 35), Mary was probably experiencing a lot of different emotions, and in all she was feeling and facing, she decided to visit Elizabeth—likely hoping to receive support, encouragement, and advice from her.[1]

Often the focus of this story of Mary visiting Elizabeth is on the blessing Elizabeth spoke over Mary when she arrived (Lk.

---

[1] Nijay K. Gupta, *Tell Her Story: How Women Led, Taught, and Ministered in the Early Church* (InterVarsity Press, 2023), 56

1:42-45). And that is a beautiful and encouraging passage of Scripture, and I'm sure it was a beautiful encouragement to Mary.

But the blessing didn't stop there!

Because Elizabeth was in the sixth month of her pregnancy when Mary visited, and because Mary stayed with Elizabeth for three months, Mary possibly witnessed the birth of John and saw Zechariah write his son's name—*Grace of God*—on a tablet. Perhaps during her stay, Zechariah communicated to her about his own encounter with an angel; maybe Elizabeth shared her own fears and uncertainties about raising a child, and her own joy and anticipation of becoming a mother; perhaps Mary heard Zechariah's prophetic song about his newborn son, and about her soon-to-be-born Son.

Mary was a young woman who needed to be seen, supported, and understood; she needed a safe place to process and cry and breathe and prepare and rejoice; she needed to be encouraged, to be believed in, and to be reminded to believe "that the Lord would fulfill what he has spoken to her!" (Lk. 1:45, CSB) And Elizabeth gave all this to her.

I love this small verse in the Christmas story, because in all I may feeling and facing during the holiday season, it encourages and reminds me: we're not made to do life alone.

—

We're not made to do life alone. I've touched on this truth in other chapters, but I think it's worth a whole chapter of it's own, because I know many of us who are single experience loneliness in our singleness. And perhaps we feel that loneliness more acutely during (or immediately after) the Christmas season.

I don't know what your holiday gatherings are like, if there's tension or conflict or estrangement among family members; if you're located close or have to travel or are unable to be with your loved ones; if there's people you're missing this year; if you've found family who aren't related to you biologically but who you celebrate with all the same; if you feel overlooked and insignificant among your siblings or cousins who are married and/or have children; if you're anxious about the dynamics of everyone coming together; or if those gatherings are times of beautiful connection for you.

But I do know this: in all you're feeling and facing, you don't have to do this alone.

At times, Jesus ministers to us in solitude. By all appearances, we are alone, yet we sense His Presence right there with us, embracing us, moving in us, filling us with joy, peace, and hope, in a way that's hard to describe and defies all logic, but that we know is real and true all the same. *Immanuel, God with Us.*

At other times, Jesus ministers to us through other people. It is their presence with us that reminds us of God's nearness; their embracing us that reminds us of our Father's love; their encouraging us that reminds us of the joy, peace, and hope Jesus gives.

We see the importance of relationships not only in Mary visiting Elizabeth, but throughout Mary's life: her and Joseph were married and raised Jesus together (Matt. 1:24-25); after their trip to the temple when Jesus was 12 years-old (Lk. 2:41-50), we don't read of Joseph being present in Jesus' adult life, while we do read of Mary's presence, so she may have been widowed by this time and stayed close to Jesus during His ministry;[2] she witnessed Jesus' death in the company of other female disciples (Jn. 19:25); while on the cross, Jesus entrusted her to His disciple John in a mother-son relationship within the new family He would form, the church (Jn. 19:26-27);[3] and she was present in the upper room, joining with the other disciples in prayer, on the day of Pentecost when they were all filled with the Holy Spirit (Acts 1:14, 2:1-4).[4]

God's design for people is that we face hardships and challenges, ask questions and seek answers, mourn and grieve, celebrate and rejoice, go about our day to day, learn and grow and become *in relationship*—relationship with God that draws ever closer, grows ever deeper, and becomes ever more intimate; and relationships with others in which we share and experience the *withness* of God.

—

[2] Gupta, *Tell Her Story*, 55

[3] Barry Danylak, *Redeeming Singleness: How the Storyline of Scripture Affirms the Single Life* (Crossway, 2010), 169

[4] Gupta, *Tell Her Story*, 66-67

Something I find so ironic about loneliness is that we're not alone in the feelings of loneliness. Your grandparent could be experiencing loneliness in their "empty nest"; your cousin who's married and has kids could be experiencing loneliness amidst the seemingly never-ending dishes to wash and diapers to change; your friend who just got engaged could be experiencing loneliness as they plan and prepare to move into a new home, a new season, a new community. So many of us experience loneliness—if not *all* of us in some way.

We're not made to do life alone. We're made for relationship. We need each other.

This too we see in the story of Mary visiting Elizabeth: in the words of blessing Elizabeth spoke over Mary, Elizabeth said, "But why am I so favored, that the mother of my Lord should come to me?" (Lk. 1:43)

Elizabeth blessed Mary, but Elizabeth also felt blessed that out of all people, Mary had come to her; Mary trusted her enough to lean on her for support, encouragement, and wisdom. And again, because of the timing of Mary's visit, she was probably a great help and comfort to Elizabeth during the final stages of her pregnancy. The blessing of relationship went both ways.

In all you're feeling and facing in your singleness this Christmas season, who could you reach out to? Who could you connect with? Who could ask for support, encouragement, and advice? Who could you support and encourage? Who could you do life with, instead of doing it alone?

Here are some ideas of ways we can reach out to others:

- Video call with a friend while wrapping presents.
- Send a "Merry Christmas" text to a few people, letting them know you're thinking of them and are grateful for them.
- Set up a time after the holidays to get together with a friend or mentor to share about your Christmas and process anything you need to with them.
- Call a friend and ask them to simply listen while you share all that's going on and how you're feeling about it.
- Get some friends together to bake Christmas cookies, take a drive to look at the Christmas lights in your town, watch a Christmas movie, or some other fun Christmas-y activity!
- Ask others to pray for and with you.

This is obviously a small list of ways we can reach out to others. But I hope these ideas give you a place to start, and perhaps spark some other ideas for you! Whatever you decide to do, don't do it alone—reach out to someone.

I know it's not the same as having a spouse. I know people don't always reciprocate or respond to our reaching out. I know the holidays are busy and schedules are full. I know it can feel overwhelming and daunting and even awkward to reach out and invite others to be with us in all we're feeling and facing.

But that's one of the beautiful things about singleness: these opportunities it gives us to reach out to others; to cultivate diverse relationships of trust, support, and intimacy; to remember that the love and care God calls us to have for one another is not confined to romance and marriage, and in fact should extend beyond marriage and biological family; and to experience, embody, and exhort the church to practice such words as these:

"Carry each other's burdens, and in this way you will fulfill the law of Christ." Galatians 6:2

"Rejoice with those who rejoice; mourn with those who mourn." Romans 12:15

"Serve one another humbly in love." Galatians 5:13

"Encourage one another daily." Hebrews 3:13

"Be kind and compassionate to one another." Ephesians 4:32

"Bear with each other and forgive one another if any of you has a grievance against someone." Colossians 3:13

"Love each other with genuine affection, and take delight in honoring each other." Romans 12:10

"In Christ we, though many, form one body, and each member belongs to all the others." Romans 12:5

"Greater love has no one than this: to lay down one's life for one's friends." John 15:13

—

When it comes to reaching out and relationships, I don't have it all figured out, and there are days when I still experience loneliness.

As you reach out and invite others in, the loneliness may linger. And that's okay. It's okay for it to be hard and it's okay for it to be awkward and it's okay for it to take time.

Relationship with God and others is the very thing for which we were created, so it makes sense that it is a deep, dynamic, and even at times difficult thing to navigate. I think we'll spend our whole lives learning and growing in how to have good, true, and beautiful relationships.

But we can trust God to provide the relationships we need. We can *ask* Him for relationships of commitment and trust and support and belonging and encouragement and intimacy—and not just of the romantic variety! And I believe as we ask and reach out and invite in, we will experience the good, true, and beautiful relationships He has for us, and we'll feel less alone and more connected in our singleness. And those around us will feel less alone in all they're feeling and facing, too.

Read Luke 1:39-45, 56

What support and encouragement did Elizabeth and Mary give to one another?

When have you experienced God's *withness* through other people?

In all you're feeling and facing, who could you reach out to?

On page 53 are ideas of ways to reach out. Is there one you want to do? Did any other ideas come to mind?

Dear Heavenly Father, thank You that even in times of loneliness, You are present with me. Thank You for caring about my relationships and for giving me these relationships that reflect Your love: _____ . I ask that You would provide for me relationships that are _____ . I love You and praise You. Amen.

Chapter 8
Hope Beyond the Deadlines

What's your favorite time of the year?

While the song may claim the Christmas season is *the most wonderful time of the year*,[1] for me, the best time of the year is October.

Here are a few reasons why: the weather is perfect for sweaters and boots, but no need for bulky jackets or hats; the colors of the leaves are vibrant reds, yellows, and oranges, a crescendoed display of beauty before they blanket the ground for its winter slumber; pumpkins and apples become key ingredients in just about every baked good and beverage; and with the cooling temperatures comes a season of coziness, a time to slow down, stay indoors, and savor stillness and simplicity.

Plus, my birthday is in October.

As much as I love celebrating my birthday (usually by enjoying all of the aforementioned fall goodness!), I can't ignore the reality that my birthday means I'm getting older.

I've never had a problem with getting older, but there have been years when I've had a problem with getting older without certain dreams coming true.

Namely, my dream of getting married.

---

[1] Andy Williams. "It's the Most Wonderful Time of the Year." *The Andy Williams Christmas Album*, Columbia Records, 1963

When I was younger, 30 was a kind of "deadline" in my head for getting married. I was (sort of) okay with being single at 22, 23, 24, as long as I was married by 30. I could be content in singleness as long as my dreams for marriage and having kids was still a possibility. I could trust God's timing and plan as long as that timing and plan included me marrying a godly (and handsome) man.

It seems naive now that I'm in my 30s and still single, but as an early-20-something, it was hard to imagine turning 30 and still being single. It felt like if I passed that "deadline" for my dreams, it would mean time was up on those dreams, and any hope that they would be fulfilled, and that my life could hold fulfillment, was gone.

In chapter 3, we talked about how it can be hard coming to the end of a year *still* single—still dreaming, still waiting, still praying, still hoping. It can also be hard entering into a new year wondering if those hopes and prayers and dreams will *ever* come true.

Maybe you have a "deadline" when it comes to your singleness and dreams and desires. Maybe that "deadline" has come and gone and you're left feeling disappointed and discouraged. Maybe you're struggling to hold onto hope for a good and beautiful future if that future doesn't hold your dreams. Maybe you're afraid to get your hopes up, because a life that's full even without fulfilled dreams seems impossible.

But what if there was a hope that lived beyond the deadlines, that carried us into each new year believing there is good in store for us, even if our dreams don't come true that year, or ever?

—

Shortly after Jesus was born, His parents took Him to the temple in Jerusalem to offer a purification sacrifice and dedicate Him to the Lord (Lk. 2:22-24). Both the sacrifice and dedication were required by the Law of Moses (Lk. 2:22-24; Lev. 12:6-8), so this wasn't an extraordinary thing for Mary and Joseph to do.

Yet while they were at the temple, there were two people who took special notice of the baby Jesus: Simeon and Anna.

Simeon is described as "righteous and devout", and he was waiting for the coming of the Messiah (Lk. 2:25).

Throughout the Old Testament, God promised a Messiah: from the prophecies of the prophets to the architecture of the temple to the rituals of the sacrificial system, all were foreshadowing and pointing to One anointed to bring the hoped for redemption, reconciliation, and restoration of creation.

The Holy Spirit had revealed to Simeon that he would not die before the Messiah came. We don't know when God gave Simeon this promise or how long he had been waiting for it to be fulfilled, but when the Holy Spirit led him to go to the temple that day, he went, and while there, he saw Jesus and recognized Him as this Promised One (Lk. 2:25-35)!

"Simeon took him in his arms and praised God, saying: Sovereign Lord, as you have promised, you may now dismiss your servant in peace. For my eyes have seen your salvation, which you have prepared in the sight of all nations: a light for revelation to the Gentiles, and the glory of your people Israel." Luke 2:28-32

Anna was a prophetess who had been married a short time when her husband died. She then lived as a widow, never leaving the temple but devoting her life to worship, prayer, and fasting. She heard the words Simeon prophesied over Jesus, and she too recognized that this Baby was the promised Messiah, and began sharing about Him to others who were waiting for God's redemption of Jerusalem (Lk. 2:36-38).

We don't know all the hopes and dreams Simeon and Anna may have held; all the different life experiences they had; all the sorrows and joys in their hearts. But we see both were looking forward with hope to the coming of the promised Messiah, and both recognized Jesus as the fulfillment of that hope and promise.

God doesn't promise us all our dreams will come true.

But there are promises He *does* give us:

- to never leave or forsake us (Heb. 13:5)
- to comfort and care for us (2 Cor. 1:3-4)
- to guide us in His will for us (Ps. 23:3)
- to provide for our needs (Phil. 4:19)
- to never stop loving us (Ps. 130:7)
- to strengthen and sustain us (2 Thes. 3:3)
- to help us resist temptation (1 Cor. 10:13)
- to give us joy and delight in Him (Ps. 16:11)
- to hear our cries (Ps. 10:17)
- and I could name even more!

2 Corinthians 1:20 tells us, "For every one of God's promises is 'Yes' in [Christ]" (CSB).

In Jesus, all God's promises find their fulfillment; all God's promises come true; all God's promises are made reality.

Because Jesus is the Messiah: the One who fulfilled all the law and prophets and completed the Father's plan for redeeming His people and restoring creation, making a way for us to be reconciled to God and live in eternal relationship with Him.

Jesus completes our joy, not our dreams. He makes us secure, not our dreams. He defines our purpose, not our dreams. He satisfies our longings, not our dreams. He meets our needs, not our dreams. He is the fulness of life, not our dreams.

Because Jesus is *our* fulfillment; not our fulfilled dreams.

So in Him, we can always have hope for a good, beautiful, and meaningful life, both today and tomorrow and forever—even when our dreams aren't coming true; even if our dreams never come true.

Because our hope is this: whether or not our dreams come true, the precious promises of Lord are true, and through them He pursues us in His love, draws us closer to Himself, and grows us in His likeness, day by day, until the day we see Him face to face.

—

But I know, in the disappointment and discouragement of unfulfilled dreams, hope can be hard to hold on to. So how do we cultivate a hope that endures beyond the deadlines?

Learn God's Promises

"Through [God's glory and goodness] he has given us his very great and precious promises." 2 Peter 1:4

We can find comfort and hope in the promises of God, because God is faithful to keep all His promises to us. Whatever this new year may hold, we can count on Him to provide, satisfy, and fulfill.

Learning God's promises isn't just about knowing them in our heads so we can recite them as a cliche when things are hard. Learning God's promises is about coming to know His heart for us and hiding His words in our hearts, so we can hold on to this truth with the assured hope that God will always be who says He will be and will always do what He says He will do.

Lean into God's Gifts

"Let all that I am praise the Lord; may I never forget the good things he does for me." Psalm 103:2, NLT

In the midst of the sorrow, frustration, and confusion of having unfulfilled dreams, it's easy to look at our lives and see only what's missing. And it's hard to believe our lives could hold joy, beauty, and purpose.

But a lack of longed-for dreams doesn't mean our lives are lacking.

Because we have a good Father who gives good gifts. And we can embrace and enjoy the gifts and goodness of our right-now lives.

As we do, there will probably still be sorrow, frustration, and confusion about our unfulfilled dreams. But right alongside them, even in the very midst of them, we can have hope and joy for all the ways God is pouring out His love to us, in us, and through us.

Look for God's Glory

"We look forward with hope to that wonderful day when the glory of our great God and Savior, Jesus Christ, will be revealed." Titus 2:13, NLT

When Scripture speaks of Jesus' return, there's a word that's often used in describing it: *glory*.

As followers of Christ, we have the hope that one day, all will be made new and whole and complete. All will be fulfilled at the wedding feast of the Lamb, when we come home to our Father who makes His dwelling with us; when we stand before the throne of the Eternal King who has vanquished sin and death (Rev. 19:6-9; 21:3-7); when we no longer see dimly, but see face to face just how beautiful and gracious and holy and good and mighty and wise our Triune God is (1 Cor. 13:12); and when there's no more doubt in our minds that we are safe in Him, that we belong with Him, that we are loved by Him (Rev. 3:5; 22:3-5).

Glory.

But this hope that we have in Christ isn't just for someday.

We have the hope that God is renewing and restoring *right now*. That He is who He is *right now*. That we are who we are in Christ *right now*.

We have been given the Holy Spirit, who is the confirmation of who and Whose we are (Rom. 8:15-16), who is the guarantee that we will inherit wholeness (Rom. 8:17; Eph. 1:14), and who is the Power that empowers us to reflect the Lord's glory in the world around us (2 Cor. 3:18).

—

Friend, I don't know what dreams you hold in your heart or what "deadlines" are in your mind about them.

But I do know that in Christ, we are promised fulfillment; from our Father, we are given gifts of His goodness; and through the Holy Spirit, we partake of and participate in the glory of the Lord.

So could you dare to hope beyond the "deadlines"? Could you dare to believe that even if your dreams die, your true Hope lives, and because He lives there is *life*—abundant, meaningful, full life —both now, and into this new year, and forever?

Read Luke 2:25-40

What promises did God fulfill in this passage?

Do you have any "deadlines" when it comes to your dreams? Even if your dreams don't come true in the way you hope, do you believe your life could still be good, beautiful, and meaningful?

What promises from God do you find comfort and joy in?

What are you looking forward to in this new year?

Dear God of Hope, thank You that in Christ, all Your promises are "Yes!" Please strengthen my hope in You and renew my hope for _____. I love You and praise You. Amen.

Chapter 9

You Matter

It was the beginning months of a new year when I went to dinner and a movie with some friends. During our chatting and catching up, one friend shared with us that she'd gone on a few dates with someone.

Everyone was excited for her and began asking her questions, interested to hear about how she'd met this date, what this person was like, and how things were going.

After several minutes, my friends then turned to me and asked, "Anything new with you?"

Based on how they communicated this question, they were more than likely really asking me, *Anything new with you in the area of dating and romance and meeting a potential romantic partner?*

There wasn't.

But since the actual question they verbalized wasn't so specific as their tone and mannerisms suggested, I decided to answer with something else that was new with me and that I was so, so, so excited about: getting to travel again to Rwanda that summer.

I'd gone on missions trips to Rwanda before, and now had another opportunity to return and serve with the same ministries, travel with some of the same teammates, and see some of the same children, families, and ministry leaders I had met before.

Traveling for ministry and for fun with friends is something I've gotten to enjoy in my singleness, and I'm grateful for the opportunities God has provided through it to learn, serve, experience new things, and see Him in other people, cultures, and countries.

So I responded to their question with joy and enthusiasm: "I'm going back to Rwanda!"

They smiled like they were happy for me, said something along the lines of "That's great!" and then promptly turned back to our friend with further questions about her date.

I felt myself deflate, all the enthusiasm and excitement sighing out of me. Whether intentionally or not (and I know these wonderful friends well enough to know it wasn't intentional), their response signaled to me that what was happening in my life didn't matter as much to them as what was happening in this friend's life, because what was happening in my life was happening within my singleness, and without dating and romance.

At times, because of things said to us, ways we're treated, and the structures and dynamics within culture, our families, and even our churches, we as single people can feel like we don't matter as much as those who are coupled.

And one of those times we can feel this is during the holidays.

And maybe in ways, we believe this: our singleness means we're inferior or incomplete in some way; as single people, our hopes, our needs, our opinions, our joys, our hardships, our growth are less significant and less worthy of support and celebration; and the thing that would give us real significance and worth would be to become *un-single*.

How do we navigate these situations, these questions and comments and conversations that seem to suggest there's something wrong with being single, and something wrong with us because we're single, these feelings of insignificance in our singleness, these beliefs that *single* means *less-than*?

—

It's a lot.

It's hard. It's frustrating. And it hurts.

There's no quick and easy fix, because there are perceptions and beliefs about singleness within the very structures of society and the church that need to be remade, and that's going to take time and the effort of many.

Yet we needn't lose heart. As we see the need and pray for and seek this remaking, in the meantime we don't have to resign ourselves to the lies that say singleness is less-than, and that we as single people are less-than.

We can, as a way of participating in this remaking in our own hearts and minds, root our own perceptions and beliefs about singleness, and about who we are as single people, in the truth of Christ.

So friend, here are three truths from God's Word I want to share with you about why your singleness doesn't mean you're inferior or incomplete, to encourage you when you're feeling this way during the holidays or any other time of year, and to participate in my own way in the remaking of the church's perceptions and beliefs about singleness:

1. Your worth isn't found in your relationship status, but in that you were created for relationship

When God created human beings, He created us *in His image*:

"Then God said, 'Let us make human beings in our image, to be like us. They will reign over the fish in the sea, the birds in the sky, the livestock, all the wild animals on the earth, and the small animals that scurry along the ground.'
"So God created human beings in his own image. In the image of God he created them; male and female he created them."
Genesis 1:26-27, NLT

The "Us" in these verses refers to the Trinity: God as Father, Son, and Holy Spirit; the Three in One eternally living in perfect union and communion with one another.

God created us to enter into communion with Him—a relationship in which we draw ever nearer, grow ever deeper, and become ever more intimate.

God also created us to be His image-bearers—to have relationships with other people in which we reflect His character (Eph. 5:1).

Being created in the image of God means we are created for relationship—in love, by love, and for love.

So it isn't a relationship status of single or dating or engaged or married or widowed or divorced or "it's complicated" that determines our worth.

It is this being made in God's image, this being created for relationship, this being loved into being, that says we already have worth.

2. *Your wholeness isn't found in romance, but in relationship with your Redeemer*

Because of sin, the image of God in us is broken, and so we are broken, because in our sin, we're separated from the relationship of intimacy with God for which we were made, and outside of this relationship, we cannot truly reflect God's righteous, holy, and glorious character in our relationships with others.

So our real need isn't a ring-on-our-finger, but a Redeemer.

This is why Jesus came! He died the death we deserve to save us from sin, so we could be made righteous and have relationship with God (1 Cor. 5:21). He rose victorious over sin and death, so we too can be raised to new life as co-heirs with Him (Eph. 2:6; Rom. 8:17). He sent His Spirit to join with our spirits and affirm that we are God's children, empowering us be imitators of Him and walk in love (Rom. 8:16; Eph. 5:1-2).

When we trust in Jesus as our Lord and Savior, all of this becomes true in our lives, and we grow in wholeness and holiness as we grow in relationship with Him.

3. *You're singleness isn't insignificant, but is a testament*

In Scripture, marriage is given the theological significance and sacredness of being a reflection of the relationship between Christ and the Church (Eph. 5:21-33).

Singleness, too, has beautiful and beneficial theological significance and sacredness.

In Luke 20:34-36, Jesus says in the New Heaven and New Earth, there won't be human marriage. There will be the wedding feast of the Lamb (Rev. 19:6-9): a relationship that is so much bigger, better, *more*; a relationship that nothing could ever surpass, because it will be complete and whole, lacking nothing. There will be joy and peace and belonging and delight and intimacy and trust and security and love in their realest, truest, most perfect forms.

This is the relationship—with our Triune God as brothers and sisters in Christ—for which we were created.

Singleness, too, is a reflection of this deep, intimate, fulfilling relationship, a testament to a covenant that is more enduring than marriage, to a love that is deeper than romance, to an intimacy that is closer than sex (1 Cor. 6:15-17).

Through Christ, we as single people (for however long we're single and even as we may still desire marriage) have the opportunity to testify to where our, to where *everyone's*, true worth, wholeness, and belonging are found: *in Christ*.

—

Yes, when those questions and comments about our singleness leave us feeling less-than, when we experience those situations in which we seem not to matter in our singleness, when we navigate those dynamics and structures that place us lower than those who are coupled, it will be hard. It will be frustrating. It will hurt.

But I believe as we more and more see our singleness and ourselves as Jesus does (and remember, Jesus lived His life on earth as a single person!), as we grow in our relationship with God and in Christ-likeness in our relationships with others, we'll be empowered by the Holy Spirit to give grace when we're upset and hurting, to have conversations with our families and friends and churches about the significance of singleness and our needs as single people, and to be a part of helping *all people* know they matter to God and have a place of belonging and significance in His family.

Read Ephesians 1:3-14

Who does this passage say you are in Christ?

Have you ever believed that singleness is less-than or that you as a single person are less-than?

What truth do you need to remember right now?

At the beginning of the chapter, I shared about a time I felt like I didn't matter because I was single; but there have been many times when others have helped me see I matter to them and to God. Describe a time when someone showed you that you matter to them.

Dear Redeemer, thank You for creating me in love and for loving me so much that You died for my sins so I could have relationship with You. Thank You that whatever my relationship status may be, I have worth, wholeness, and significance in Christ. Please help to remember this truth: _____. I love You and praise You. Amen.

Chapter 10
More than Enough

There have been many Christmases when, as I was hanging ornaments on my tree, eating oyster stew with my family, watching the children of my church act out that very first Christmas, or doing any other holiday preparations or activities, there would be this stirring inside me.

But it wasn't a stirring of joy or peace or wonder at the good news we're celebrating.

Rather, it was a restless, distracting stirring of discontentment. Discontentment that I was celebrating this season single rather than married.

Throughout much of my 20s, I struggled with deep discontentment in my singleness. Even in times of happiness, fun, and wonder, there was still this undercurrent of dissatisfaction with my relationship status that pulled at me and kept me from fully immersing myself in the joy, goodness, and purpose that was all around me.

Often, this undercurrent tugged at my mind and heart in the form of a little thought: *If only I were married...*

If only I were married, if only I was enjoying this time, facing this hardship, walking this path with a spouse, then my life—even the good things in my life—would be more meaningful, have more purpose, hold more happiness, be more fun.

And the Christmas season wasn't any different.

While I absolutely love Christmas (it is my favorite holiday!) and find so much delight in the traditions, preparations, gatherings, and festivities, there were still these restless *if onlys* that said this wonderful, beautiful, meaningful season would hold *even more* wonder, beauty, and meaning *if only I was married.*

If only I was observing the traditions, making the preparations, going to the gatherings, and enjoying the festivities with a spouse by my side.

Friend, do you sense this, too? This undercurrent of discontentment tugging at your own heart and mind with whispers and pictures of how this season would be more wonderful, less lonely, more meaningful, less stressful, more joyful, less hard, more fun, less…, more… *if only you were married*?

Christmas is a celebration of the greatest gift given. And I'm thinking we'd all like to celebrate this gift without the *if onlys* of discontentment saying our experience of this gift is less-than or lacking because we're single.

Because it isn't.

—

Christmas is a celebration of the greatest gift given:

"Today in the town of David a Savior has been born to you; he is the Messiah, the Lord." Luke 2:11

Jesus was born in the town of David, called Bethlehem. Bethlehem was a small town in the hill country of Judea, known primarily as a place for sheep and shepherds.[1] Why would this be the place for the Savior of the world to be born?

700 years before Jesus' birth,[2] the prophet Micah prophesied the Messiah would come out of this nondescript town:

"But you, Bethlehem Ephrathah,
  though you are small among the clans of Judah,
out of you will come for me
  one who will be ruler over Israel,
whose origins are from of old,

---

[1] Kaitlin Febles, *Bethlehem: Little Town, Big Significance*, The Gospel Coalition, 2021, https://www.thegospelcoalition.org/article/bethlehem-little-town-big-significance/

[2] Kay Arthur, *Discover the Bible for Yourself* (Harvest House Publishers, 2000), 28-31

from ancient times." Micah 5:2

Micah goes on to describe how this Ruler would protect, deliver, and care for His people as a shepherd does his sheep (Mic. 5:3-6).

The Hebrew word *Bethlehem* means "house of bread."[3] As God was leading His people from Egypt and to the promised land, He promised to provide for them in a miraculous way:

"I will rain down bread from heaven for you." Exodus 16:4

Each day, God sent enough manna for His people to eat so they would not go hungry in the desert (Ex. 16:1-31).

In John 6:35, Jesus makes this declaration:

"I am the bread of life. Whoever comes to me will never be hungry, and whoever believes in me will never be thirsty."

The physical bread God sent to meet the needs of His people was a foreshadowing of His sending His Son, whose life would provide for our need of salvation in a miraculous way (Jn. 6:32-58).

In John 10:11, Jesus makes another declaration:

"I am the good shepherd. I lay down my life for my sheep."

In fact, throughout the Gospel of John, Jesus makes seven such "I Am" statements:

- "I am the bread of life." (Jn. 6:35)
- "I am the light of the world." (Jn. 8:12)
- "I am the gate for the sheep." (Jn. 10:7)
- "I am the good shepherd." (Jn. 10:11, 14)
- "I am the resurrection and the life." (Jn. 11:25)
- "I am the way and the truth and the life." (Jn. 14:6)
- "I am the true vine." (Jn. 15:1)

---

[3] Febles, *Bethlehem*, https://www.thegospelcoalition.org/article/bethlehem-little-town-big-significance/

From a town of shepherds comes our Good Shepherd to "seek and save the lost" (Luk. 19:10). From a town of sheep comes the Lamb of God who is the way for our salvation, purification, and resurrection (Jn. 1:29; 1 Pet. 1:18-21; Rev. 7:9-10, 7:17, 12:11, 19:7-9, 22:1). From a town called *House of Bread* comes the Bread of Life who nourishes and satisfies our every need and longing (Is. 55:1-3).

In His seven "I Am" statements, Jesus declares Himself to be the One who loves and cares for us; who provides a place of security and belonging; who is our light in the darkness; who shows us the way and makes the way for us; who nourishes and strengthens us; who gives us not just surviving-life, but life that is abundant and never-ending and lacking nothing.

These statements are powerful not just in the imagery Jesus uses as He describes Himself—as He says "This is who I am"—but also in the fact that He says "I Am."

This is an echo of the name God identified Himself by to His people as He delivered them from slavery in Egypt, re-established His covenant with them, and gave them the law:

"God said to Moses, 'I am who I am. This is what you are to say to the Israelites: "I am has sent me to you."'" Exodus 3:14

In declaring this name, God declares He is self-existent, and all life and breath come from Him. He declares He is eternal and unchanging, and so will always be good to His people and faithful to His promises. He declares He lacks for nothing, and is all-sufficient for everything.[4]

Jesus, as God incarnate, makes this same declaration:

"I tell you the truth, before Abraham was even born, I am!" John 8:58

Jesus is not just one option out of many. *He Is.* Jesus is not an add-on to our idea of the good life. *He Is.* Nothing is *more* than Him. *He Is.*

And because of who Jesus is—*I Am*—and who He is to us, for us, and in us—our Good Shepherd, our Door, our Light, our Way, our Truth, our Bread, our True Vine, our Resurrected Life—

---

[4] Kay Arthur, *Lord, I Want to Know You* (Multnomah Books, 1992), 63-64

Christmas is not less-than or lacking when celebrated as a celebration of who He is. Singleness is not less-than or lacking when lived in relationship with Him.

—

I've found that when I'm thinking those *if only* thoughts, it's an indication that I need to examine where I'm looking for my joy and wholeness; where I'm turning for my strength and security; what I'm believing will fulfill and satisfy me.

What is your source?

In my mid-twenties, as I was going through a bit of a quarter-life crises, the discontentment I felt about being single reached an all-time high. I also began experiencing heightened anxiety and depression during this time.

I began going to therapy and during one session, I told my therapist, "I feel like I just want *more*."

In typical therapist fashion, she asked me, "What do you mean by *more*?"

And as I sat there on my therapist's couch, it hit me: I was believing marriage was the *more*.

Through those conversations in therapy, conversations with other wise and encouraging people in my life, and conversations with God in prayer, God convicted me that I was looking to my dreams of marriage and motherhood as the source of my joy, peace, worth, and wholeness.

But all these are found in Christ:

"I have told you this so that my joy may be in you and that your joy may be complete." John 15:11

"So you also are complete through your union with Christ." Colossians 2:10, NLT

"Even before he made the world, God loved us and chose us in Christ to be holy and without fault in his eyes." Ephesians 1:4, NLT

"Peace I leave with you; my peace I give you. I do not give to you as the world gives. Do not let your hearts be troubled and do not be afraid." John 14:27

I know, *I know*, that singleness can be hard, sad, frustrating, confusing, stressful, wearisome, lonely, and more. And I'll be the first to tell you it's okay to acknowledge these hard things and let ourselves feel these heavy emotions.

But when we look to marriage as the remedy for this hard and heavy stuff, we're making it an idol. Because we're looking to it as the source of our peace, our joy, our comfort, our security, our fulfillment, when we should be looking to Jesus: our Peace amidst the stress, our Strength under the burdens, our Friend in the loneliness, our Comfort in the sadness, our Joy in the mundane, our Truth in the confusion, our Delight in the longings.

This was something I had to confess and repent of, and I am continually learning to more and more abide in Jesus as my Source.

When our Source is Christ, singleness isn't empty of joy, peace, hope, purpose, and wholeness. Because *Jesus is* our joy, peace, hope, purpose, and wholeness.

What sustains you?

One of the things my therapist talked with me about was possible reasons I could be experiencing discontentment in my singleness. As I shared above, one of those reasons was that I was trying to find joy and contentment through something other than Jesus.

Another reason she shared was that the discontentment could also be God stirring a restlessness in my heart because He had something new for me to step into.

I had been framing my dreams for my future around marriage for so long, but perhaps God was inviting me into a new dream. Not necessarily one that would replace my dream for marriage, but one that was just as good and purposeful, and that didn't have to wait for marriage for me to pursue.

Maybe the restless stirring in your heart at the end of this year is just that: God is calling you into something new. As a new year begins, perhaps there is something else He has for you to learn, to experience, to do, to become. That new thing could be marriage, or it could be something else that is also good and purposeful!

But maybe we don't believe we can do that thing or step into that newness or experience that goodness in our singleness, without a romantic partner by our side. *Maybe we don't want to.*

Because having a romantic partner by our side is what we've believed will sustain us through the challenges and fears; it's what we've believed will give us the courage and wisdom needed; it's what we've believed will bring purpose to daily living.

In Philippians 4, the apostle Paul writes:

"I know how to live on almost nothing or with everything. I have learned the secret of living in every situation, whether it is with a full stomach or empty, with plenty or little. For I can do everything through Christ, who gives me strength… And this same God who takes care of me will supply all your needs from his glorious riches, which have been given to us in Christ Jesus." Philippians 4:12-13, 19, NLT

With Jesus, we already have all we need to step into whatever God has for us! He is the One who sustains us in both the opportunities and challenges of something new, and in the day-in and day-out of daily life.

What brings you satisfaction?

I was believing marriage was the more; the *more* that would make the hard more manageable and the good even better; the *more* that would fill the holiday season with all the joy, fun, and love the songs sing about and the movies portray; the *more* that would finally be *enough* for me to be satisfied and content.

And this belief, this thinking *if only I were married*, kept me from fully leaning into, embracing, and enjoying the presence of God *already with me.*

Because marriage doesn't make God's presence more near. Marriage doesn't make God's goodness better. Marriage doesn't make His love richer or His care more complete or His provision more adequate or His grace more sufficient. Marriage doesn't make God *more.*

He Is.

Do we believe this? Do we believe Jesus is enough? Do we believe He fulfills and satisfies?

Or do we believe we need something *more*?

Instead of thinking *If only I were married...*, let's delight in Jesus! Let's worship Him. Let's enjoy His goodness and His good gifts to us. Let's celebrate the greatest gift given: the gift of God's Son, in whom we have grace, salvation, joy, hope, forgiveness, peace, righteousness, new life, purpose, belonging, sonship, and *so much more.*

And let's fully lean into this *more* with wholehearted abandon, a trust fall into our Father's mighty, loving, safe arms.

"All praise to God, the Father of our Lord Jesus Christ, who has blessed us with every spiritual blessing in the heavenly realms because we are united with Christ." Ephesians 1:3, NLT

"I have come that they may have life, and have it to the full." John 10:10

Jesus is our Good Shepherd—we lack nothing.

Jesus is our nourishing bread—we are not empty.

Jesus is our true and resurrected life—we have *more* than enough.

Read the seven "I Am" statements of Jesus: John 6:35; John 8:12; John 10:7; John 10:11, 14; John 11:25; John 14:6; John 15:1

Is there a particular "I Am" statement that resonates with you in this season?

What "if only" thoughts do you have?

What have you been looking to as the source of your joy, peace, worth, purpose, strength, wisdom, courage, and wholeness? How could you look to Jesus instead?

Dear Jesus, I praise You for who You are: the Great I Am. When discontentment stirs, please help me to remember that You are _____. Please fill me with Your joy and peace. I love You and praise You. Amen.

Chapter 11
The Joy of Christmas

In the writing, teaching, and ministry I do, both online and in my local church and friendships, I often think of myself as an "advocate for joyful singleness."

After all the previous chapters, I'm sure it goes without saying, but I'm gonna say it anyways: this doesn't mean I think we have to enjoy every aspect of singleness or can't have a desire for marriage.

It means I believe that in Christ, we can live joyfully in singleness and lean into the goodness of singleness, for however long we're single, even as we may hope and long for marriage. And I want to help other singles believe in and experience this joyful, purposeful, beautiful way of being Jesus offers us in relationship with Himself.

I may be an "advocate for joyful singleness", but as I shared in the previous chapter, I didn't always have joy in my singleness.

If 10 years ago you would have told me I'd still be single at 34, I would have cried tears of sorrow and hopelessness. *Please, dear God, let it not be true.*

If 10 years ago you also would have told me I'd actually be content, be proud of myself, be filled with joy and hope and gratitude in still being single at 34, I would have laughed incredulously. *Yeah, right.*

But deep in my heart, I would have also asked, *How?* How could I have such joy in singleness when singleness isn't what I wanted?

In a word: *Jesus.*

That's really what all of what we've talked about comes back to: Jesus, Jesus, Jesus.

And amidst all the decorating and baking and shopping and gathering and eating and gift-giving, that's really what we're celebrating: Jesus, Jesus, Jesus.

Joy is found all throughout the Gospel tellings of the first Christmas, but I think sometimes we need to remember this joy. That this joy wasn't just for that first Christmas, it's part of every Christmas, even when a particular Christmas season holds heartache. This joy isn't just for celebrations, but for day to day life, even when day to day life is lonely, tiring, or boring. This joy isn't just for someday when hopes and dreams come true, but for today, even when we're discouraged, sad, frustrated, confused, and overwhelmed.

And sometimes, we need to intentionally lean into this joy, this good news that the yearly rhythm of Christmas invites us to remember and rejoice in.

But, *how?*

—

After God delivered His people from slavery in Egypt, He led them to camp at the base of Mount Sinai for a period of time. During this time, God renewed the covenant He had made with Abraham, Isaac, and Jacob, now establishing it with the entire nation of Israel.[1]

Part of this covenant renewal was the giving of the law, in which God instructed His people on what living in covenant relationship with Him and one another was to look like in day to day life, and in which He gave His promises of blessing should the people walk faithfully in this covenant, and warnings of judgement should they choose to be unfaithful and forsake the Lord their God.[2]

Included in the law were instructions for regular feasts, from the Passover Celebration to the Feast of Weeks to the Day of Atonement. These feasts were to be times throughout the year,

---

[1] Barry Danylak, *Redeeming Singleness: How the Storyline of Scripture Affirms the Single Life* (Crossway, 2010), 56

[2] Danylak, *Redeeming Singleness*, 56-57

connected to the rhythm of the seasons and Israel's history, that the people were to celebrate as a way of remembering and rejoicing in who God is, all He had done for them, and the covenant relationship they shared with Him (Lev. 23:1-44).

And while the people didn't know it (but perhaps in a way sensed it), these feasts, along with the whole of the law, pointed to and foreshadowed something more: Jesus, who through His birth, life, death, and resurrection fulfilled the law and prophets (Matt. 5:17; Rom. 3:21-31; Gal. 3:8-4:7; Heb. 8:1-10:18).

As the early Church grew, more and more Gentiles (non-Jewish people) began following Jesus, and the Church began implementing celebrations and yearly rhythms that were different from (though sometimes still linked to) those Old Testament feasts.[3] We now have the church calendar, with various holidays and celebrations depending on your church tradition, that we celebrate to remember and rejoice in who God is, all He has done for us through Jesus, the new covenant relationship we have with Him in Christ's blood, and the assured hope of Jesus' return as our King and Bridegroom.

The two major holidays on this calendar that many church traditions celebrate are the Lenten and Easter season, and the season of Advent and Christmas.

During this season, Christmas is a yearly invitation to intentionally and communally remember and rejoice in the birth of Christ; that God gave us the gift of salvation, newness, and belonging not in a prettily wrapped package, but *in Himself.*

In Luke 2, after finding no place in Bethlehem to stay but a stable, giving birth and laying her new Baby in a manger, and being visited by shepherds who had been visited by angels, verse 19 tells us, "Mary treasured up all these things and pondered them in her heart."

All the events of that eventful day Mary tucked into her memory, to remember and reflect on throughout her life (Lk. 4:19, NLT). As the Boy Jesus "grew in wisdom and stature" (Lk. 2:52); after He went missing and she found Him in the temple and He asked her, "Didn't you know I had to be in my Father's house?" (Lk. 2:41-49); as she witnessed Him turn water into wine (Jn. 2:1-11); when she and His siblings came to Him and He said,

---

[3] Phylicia Masonheimer, *Seasonal Celebrations: Your Guide to Celebrating the Gospel Through Church Holidays* (Every Woman a Theologian, 2022), 27-30, 56

"Anyone who does the will of my Father in heaven is my brother and sister and mother!" (Lk. 12:46-50, NLT); as she heard of Him healing the sick and giving sight to the blind and raising the dead (Lk. 7:22); when she stood at the foot of the cross and heard Him cry out, "My God, my God, why have you forsaken me?" (Matt. 27:46) and watched Him die; when she heard the unbelievable news that the tomb was empty and her Son and Lord was alive again; as she prayed in the upper room and was filled with the Holy Spirit (Acts 1:14, 2:1-4)[4]... I'm sure through it all, she was remembering those memories, pondering them in her heart, reflecting on what it all meant.

Each Christmas is a time for us to treasure and ponder; to treasure and ponder what the incarnation means for us and how we are called us to live in light of this good news of great joy, that a Savior has been born.

There are many ways we can treasure and ponder the true meaning of Christmas:

- Perhaps we sit to read of that first Christmas with fresh eyes and an open heart.
- Perhaps we slow down to engage in meaningful traditions that celebrate Jesus' birth and focus our hearts and minds on what Christmas is really all about.
- Perhaps we pause to breathe and notice the presence of God with us.
- Perhaps we still ourselves amidst the festivities to take in the beauty and blessings around us, often in the form the people with us.
- Perhaps we end our day without noise or screens, but with silence to ponder and reflect on whatever God may want to show us, teach us, and grow in us from that day.

While perhaps some of the child-like magic and wonder and fun of the season fades over the years, the more we celebrate Christmas as a celebration of the birth of Jesus, the more this "magic" is revealed to be the wondrous mystery of God become flesh; the more this wonder deepens into worship of an Almighty

---

[4] Nijay K. Gupta, *Tell Her Story: How Women Led, Taught, and Ministered in the Early Church* (InterVarsity Press, 2023), 55

King becoming a helpless babe; the more the festive fun becomes a joyful sharing in the presence of *Immanuel, God with us*.

—

Joy is found throughout the Christmas story.

One of my favorite places in the Christmas story where we find joy is in Luke 1:46-55, a passage often titled "Mary's Song".[5] And what a beautiful song it is!

It opens with these words:

"My soul glorifies the Lord, and my spirit rejoices in God my Savior." Luke 1:46-47

Mary goes on to sing of God's salvation, compassion, blessing, might, holiness, mercy, faithfulness, omniscience, sovereignty, and care, both in covenant with His people and in her own life.[6]

That's something I love about this song, how personal and intimate it is:

"For he has been mindful of the humble state of his servant... for the Mighty One has done great things for me—holy is his name." Luke 1:48-49

This song resembles other songs found in the Old Testament, echoing the words of women who had gone before: Miriam after God led His people through the parted waters of the Red Sea and destroyed the army of the nation that had enslaved them (Ex. 14:15-15:21); Deborah after God gave His people triumph in battle and brought victory through the hands of a woman (Jdg. 4:4-5:31); Hannah after God answered her prayers for a child and she dedicated her son to the Lord (1 Sam. 1:1-2:10).[7]

These "hymns of divine victory"[8] sing of how God was faithful to His covenant, gave victory against all odds, and accomplished the seemingly impossible through ordinary people.

---

[5] Such as the *New International Version* (copyright 1973, 1978, 1984, 2011 by Biblica, Inc.)

[6] Gupta, *Tell Her Story*, 53

[7] Gupta, *Tell Her Story*, 53

[8] Gupta, *Tell Her Story*, 53

Now Mary joins in this song of victory that echos through the ages of God's mightiness to save, power to redeem, trustworthiness to provide, and faithfulness to love.

We, too, can join in this victory song, rejoicing in God our Savior, trusting His mindfulness of us, worshiping Him in His holiness, and thanking Him for the wonderful things He has done for us.

This song Mary sang seems to be a happy one, springing from a time of happiness.

But I sometimes I wonder exactly how Mary sang this song. Was it with a bright smile on her face and happiness in her heart? Or was it a bold declaration in the face of fear? Or perhaps it was a whispered prayer of faith? Or maybe it was sung through tears as she clung to God and called on Him for help?

Because sometimes, rejoicing doesn't look like smiles and happiness and serenity. Sometimes, rejoicing is done through tears, in the face of fears, in the midst of uncertainty. Because rejoicing is taking joy and delight in who God is—that *He is* my joy, my hope, my peace, my strength, my comfort, my help—and that He is with me always. Who He is doesn't change depending on the circumstances we find ourselves in or the emotions we find ourselves experiencing, and this is why we can "rejoice in the Lord always" (Phil. 4:4).

Another title that's been given to this song is *Mary's Magnificat*. *Magnificat* is from the Latin word for "magnify", from the first line of the song:[9]

"My soul magnifies the Lord." Luke 1:46, CSB

This is what rejoicing does: it magnifies the Lord.

Not that it makes Him *more* good, *more* loving, *more* mighty, *more* faithful, *more* of who He is. Nothing can make God *more*.

But rejoicing fixes our gaze on Jesus. It focuses our hearts and minds on His goodness, His love, His mightiness, His faithfulness, His *more-than-enoughness*. So we become *more* aware of and present to and able to delight in His presence in our lives.

This is why, whatever the year may have held and whatever the next year brings, we celebrate Christmas, why we take this

---

[9] "magnificat", *Merriam-Webster.com*, 2025, https://www.merriam-webster.com/dictionary/magnificat

time to remember and rejoice in the birth of Christ: because it magnifies the Lord—both in that He is worthy of all glory, honor, and praise; and in that it re-centers us in relationship with Him, to orient our days, our decisions, our priorities, our daily routines and rhythms around His presence with us, in us, and through us.

—

There is Someone who calls us *His*.

There is Someone we can call *mine*.

This is the joy—and the peace, hope, wonder, goodness, and meaning—of Christmas: Jesus was born, coming to be with us so we could be with Him.

And this is the joy—and the peace, hope, wonder, goodness, and meaning—of singleness: the *withness* of God, in whom we have relationship and presence and communion and belonging and intimacy and commitment and love that is not less-than or lacking, but whole and rich, abundant and abounding, filling and overflowing; and that singleness is a testimony to the *enoughness* of this *withness*, an invitation for the Church to be a family in which the *withness* of God is experienced and shared, and a foreshadowing of eternity lived in covenant relationship with Christ as His bride.

Let's lean into this joy. Let's celebrate this Christmas. Let's live in relationship with our God who is with us.

Read Luke 1:46-55. You could also read Miriam's song in Exodus 15:20-21; Deborah's song in Judges 5:1-31; and Hannah's song in 1 Samuel 2:1-10.

What reasons does Mary (and these other women) give for her rejoicing?

On page 82 are some ideas of ways to treasure and ponder the true meaning of Christmas. Are there any you would like to do this Christmas season?

Dear Lord, my soul glorifies You and my spirit rejoices in You, for You are my _____. I worship You because You are _____. Thank You for these great things You have done for me: _____. I love You and praise You. Amen.

A Final Note of Encouragement

Each Christmas, my Pappaw (maternal grandfather) would dress up like Santa Clause to hand us grandkids our stockings. As everyone opened their presents, he was usually the first to throw a wad of wrapping paper at some unsuspecting family member. And as soon as the gift-giving was finished, he and Mammaw would start making oyster stew for dinner, a generations-old family tradition Pappaw took pride in carrying on. (And I'm glad he did, because trust me, it's delicious!)

This Christmas will be my family's first Christmas without him.

I know this Christmas is going to be hard. I know there will be many moments of sadness and lots of tears shed as we continue to grieve. But I also know there will be sweet and special moments, and so much laughter even through tears, as we remember, celebrate, and continue to make memories together.

Because we have this hope: Pappaw is with Jesus. He's experiencing in fullness the *withness* of God. The *withness* that God desires with each one of us, so much so that He sent His Son to be born to us, to live with us and die for us, and to be raised to life to give us new life in Him.

Revelation 21:3-4 gives us this promise:

"Look, God's home is now among his people! He will live with them, and they will be his people. God himself will be with them. He will wipe every tear from their eyes, and there will be no more

death or sorrow or crying or pain. All these things are gone forever." NLT

While Christmas is a time of remembering Jesus' birth, it's also a time of looking forward to His return as our King and Bridegroom, when He will "make all things new" (Rev. 21:5, NKJV).

Life happens in seasons, both literally and in more intangible ways.

We're currently in the holiday season, then a new year will come. After that, where I live in the northern hemisphere, winter will give way to the newness of spring, then summer will bring longer days and warmer temperatures, then fall will come with the changing colors of the leaves, then winter will arrive, and we'll be in another Christmas season once again.

There are also seasons of life. Seasons of change, of growth, of stillness, of plenty, of want, of silence, of breakthrough, of loss, of hardship, of healing, of grief, of celebration, of rest.

Some of us will be single for only some of these seasons, some of us for many seasons, some of us for our whole lives, and some will after a time of marriage find themselves single again.

In all these seasons, there is something constant. Or rather, *Someone.*

I'm thinking you already know who He is: our Triune God. Our Heavenly Father, our Savior Jesus, our Advocate the Holy Spirit.

He will be with me and my family as we navigate this holiday season without my Pappaw. And He will be with you in whatever you're navigating this Christmas.

He is with us in every season, drawing us closer to Himself, rooting us deeper in His love, and growing us more in His likeness.

And someday, all these seasons of life will be engulfed by eternal life, when we shall see our God face to face and experience in fullness His *withness*, not for a season but forever.

It's gonna be glorious.

Now before we end, could I pray for you?

Dear Heavenly Father,

We come to You with grateful hearts. Thank You for the ways You have met with us, revealed Yourself to us, and drawn us closer to You. And thank You for the ways You will continue to do so.

I lift up to You the one reading this, in whatever season of life they are in, and however they may be feeling about being single in this season. Please continue to remind them of Your heart for them —how You see them, love them, and care for them.

Please give them a blessed Christmas season and fill them with the comfort and joy of knowing You are with them always.

We thank You for Your presence and Your promises. Draw near to us as we draw near to you.

Amen.

About the Author

Jessica Faith Hagen is a writer and speaker who shares biblical encouragement and advice to help fellow singles know their worth in Christ, navigate singleness with joy, and live wholeheartedly for Jesus.

When she's not writing, you'll find her reading a good book, going for a walk, or baking something sweet.

Find more encouragement and connect with Jessica online @jessicafaithwrites and on her website theoverflowing.com.

Also by Jessica Faith Hagen:

Dear Single Girl: 30 Days for Seeing Yourself and Your Singleness as Jesus Does

Dear Single Girl Guided Journal: 30 Bible Readings and Journaling Prompts for Rooting Your Heart in Truth

Come: a Journaling Journey through the Life of Jesus

Wonderful: a Devotional Journal for the Christmas Season

Bibliography

Kay Arthur. *Lord, I Want to Know You.* Multnomah Books, 1992

Kay Arthur. *Discover the Bible for Yourself.* Harvest House Publishers, 2000

Barry Danylak. *Redeeming Singleness: How the Storyline of Scripture Affirms the Single Life.* Crossway, 2010

H. Ray Dunning. *Reflecting the Divine Image: Christian Ethics in Wesleyan Perspective.* Wipf and Stock Publishers, 1998

Kaitlin Febles. *Bethlehem: Little Town, Big Significance.* The Gospel Coalition, 2021. https://www.thegospelcoalition.org/article/bethlehem-little-town-big-significance/

Margaret Feinberg. *Spark Your Joy: A 4-Week Advent Bible Study Devotional.* Margaret Feinberg, 2014

Jazmin N. Frank. *Women of the Covenant: Discovering God's Faithfulness to Women in a Broken and Hurting World.* Beautifully Devoted Resources, 2021

Nijay K. Gupta. *Tell Her Story: How Women Led, Taught, and Ministered in the Early Church.* InterVarsity Press, 2023

Phylicia Masonheimer. *Seasonal Celebrations: Your Guide to Celebrating the Gospel Through Church Holidays.* Every Woman a Theologian, 2022

Frank More. *The Holy Spirit.* The Foundry Publishing, 2023

Samuel M. Powell. *The Trinity.* The Foundry Publishing, 2020

Ann Spangler, Jean E. Syswerda. *Women of the Bible: A One-Year Devotional Study of Women in Scripture.* Zondervan, 2007

James Strong. *The New Strong's Expanded Exhaustive Concordance of the Bible.* Thomas Nelson Publishers, 2010

Danielle Treweek. *The Meaning of Singleness: Retrieving an Eschatological Vision for the Contemporary Church.* InterVarsity Press, 2023

Andy Williams. "It's the Most Wonderful Time of the Year." *The Andy Williams Christmas Album*, Columbia Records, 1963

What were Isreal's 400 years of silence? Got Questions Ministries, 2016. http://www.compellingtruth.org/400-years-of-silence.html

"magnificat" Def. *Merriam-Webster.com*, 2025. https://www.merriam-webster.com/dictionary/magnificat

www.ingramcontent.com/pod-product-compliance
Lightning Source LLC
Chambersburg PA
CBHW072045040426
42447CB00012BB/3024